Receptive to Fire

College City Publications
Northfield, Minnesota

Also by B Wardlaw

Coca-Cola Anarchist (2010)

B WARDLAW

Receptive to Fire

With "The Voice of Script,"
A Commentary by Ed Powell

Drawings by Christopher Coffey

© Copyright 2015 by B Wardlaw
All rights reserved.

First printing: December 2010
Second printing: March 2012
Third printing (with revisions): April 2013
Fourth printing (with revisions): September 2013
Fifth printing (with revisions): May 2015

No part of this book may be reproduced in any form, by photostat, microfilm, xerography, or any means, or incorporated into any information retrieval system,
electronic or mechanical, without the written permission
of the copyright owner.

All inquiries and comments can be addressed to:

E-mail: bwardlawcca@gmail.com
Web site: http://Receptivetofire.com

Acknowledgments and Credits —

    Drawings: Christopher Coffey, www.cloudsandsea-france.com

    Editing, Design, and Production: Nancy Ashmore,
    Ashmore Ink, Northfield, MN, www.ashmoreink.com.

International Standard Book No.: 978-0-9797423-8-5

Printed in the United States of America

Keywords: Poetry, epic poems, evolution theory, quantum theory, Christianity, rise of civilization, Greece, Rome

CONTENTS

     FOREWORD

2   PART ONE: PRE-HISTORY

12 PART TWO: EARLY "CIVILIZATIONS"

24 PART THREE: GREECE

42 PART FOUR:
      ROME, JOSHUA OF NAZARETH, THE "DARK AGES"

52 PART FIVE: A RENAISSANCE

70 EPILOGUE: OUR "MODERN AGE"

76 "THE VOICE OF SCRIPT" —
      ED POWELL'S COMMENTARY ON *FIRE*

112 ENDNOTES

117 GLOSSARY

122 AN EXCERPT FROM *COCA-COLA ANARCHIST*,
      THE STORY BEHIND THE CREATION OF
      RECEPTIVE TO FIRE

FOREWORD

Receptive to Fire explores steps in human evolution. In many places at many times, it uncovers encouraging signs that we still might evolve in positive ways (perhaps even survive as a species) if we come to understand something of our deep history. In *Fire* you'll find invented characters — Neurod [**Nēu-rod**], Hurabo [**Who-rāh-bo**], Bahdawils [**Bāh-dah-wils**], Semeuse [**Saymōōs**], Wanshee [**Wān-she**] — who, with Zarathustra and Siddhartha (based loosely on historical figures) and with my narrator, live throughout the work. All, in part, are intended as archetypes and as allegorical. I hope they are true to life, to the spirit of their times, and to a sense of place which, like my imagined villages of Arzen and Simrand, live *beyond* time along with two major "characters," an astounding sleek-black Doe and a high-flying Seabird.

Dr. Powell's profound 1983 commentary, "The Voice of Script," enhanced enormously my appreciation of history and historical research; I hope it will do the same for you. And if you're troubled by unfamiliar names and events in reading either "Script" or *Fire*, the glossary at the back of the book might — in some cases — be helpful.

For those of you who are, in general, intimidated by poetry, DON'T BE. As with much poetry, these sonnets are perhaps best read as "prose," i.e., from sentence to sentence rather than from line to line, and each stanza may be read as a paragraph connected to the others. Hoping that rhythms and rhymes will come naturally, I suggest you react to punctuation just as you would in reading anything else. Words such as "flower," "power," "tower," and "toward," may sometimes be heard as one-syllable, sometimes as two.

And if you're inclined, please email bwardlawcca@gmail.com and share your thoughts about this book.

In memory of Ed Powell (1925-2001) and his zest for life.

And in memory of my son Shepard (1969-1990)
who inspired in me the feeling — *still* generated by
my daughter Julia — that life is worth living.

And in appreciation for the love of two women,
Susan and Patricia,
each of whom tolerated me for a
quarter of a century as a compañero.

Receptive to Fire is dedicated to the boys and girls,
women and men — throughout history — who have been
seduced into the sufferings of war . . .
and to the boys and girls, women and men
who have resisted that seduction.

PART ONE: PRE-HISTORY

1

From sea to land to tree we made our way,
Bright gentle ape, great graceful swinging ape,
Now comes our day to — free in tree-tops! — sway.
While predators crawl low we find escape,
Race with a rising sun above the earth
Untilled, sing at a feast of nuts and fruit.
Attaining new perspectives, *sing*. Well worth
A climb are highest limbs, the tender shoot,
Our chance to ride this crest of Time's vast wave
In strength and courage, past all need to kill:
One family in overcoming. Rave,
Most jealous Chaos. Bend to this new will.
    Remembrance mixed with power to forget;
    A dawn of peace, our primal scene's been set.

2

How came it then, the Great Wave bursting down?
We wakened, wondering, on strange damp ground,
Awake from sea-dreams, fears that we would drown.
(Promethean failure would have *kept* us bound!)
Had changing weather wilted leaves and fruit?
Had sly new killers crept into our trees?
Or were we mesmerized into pursuit
Of distant tones? Our mind past reason sees.
Alert, we wander now both beach and plains,
But claws, sharp claws and fangs . . . we're chased without cease
And struggle to transcend new hunger pains
And question, "Was it real, remembered peace?"
    We scavenge, run, hot blood on trembling hands;
    No mother soothes, no father understands.

3

Reflective light in caves, our eyes ablaze
(Praise brave Prometheus!), Fire's trapped and held
For warmth and safety, light at night, but still a maze
Of need we see, persistent need to weld
Survival in a world that doesn't care.
Help — fickle world — Help me — Not spoken yet.
Fire's gifts bring hope, and yet . . . Where are we? *Where?*
Fierce predators still howl. Hold moon. Don't set!
From death, from dreamed of and remembered doom,
Will we be saved? Ah, yes. Life-bearing Sun
Comes pushing — Ah — out from its grave, our gloom,
To rise, to plot once more the race we'll run.
    Auummmm. Blazing Sunlight . . . dread Night's weight gives way.
    Auummmm. Blazing Sunlight . . . guide our trip today.

4

Moving, always moving, desperate, homeless,
Lost ones — Me — hunger foremost — Food — small one
Hanging helpless, dead . . . dead! Where, Mate, is closeness?
Help! — Our group must hunt or die now. Run. Run!
Blood-lust hunt to kill, to live. Compulsive hunt
And run and kill with, cross a valley,
New words — Look! — screamed over — Kill! — reluctant,
Urgent cry to run and kill though weary,
Sick, that others' pain is turned to quivering meat,
The price of life for us. Save family!
Starvation foiled, surviving children eat,
So sleep, my Love, and dream of harmony:
    High-swinging safe-day, ripe fruit hanging there
    Again — dream swirl — and flowers in your hair.

5

Entranced, one moment, by the face, my face
(Yet yours) aglimmer in a pond of ice,
An image, clear dimensions fit to trace
Our journey. Birth's red morn to death's night splice.
Transparent, candid ice . . . turn . . . Crash! The gift
Of rare serenity is split, thick ice
By lightning torn, our image torn and rift,
And I'm adrift . . . Such cowardly retreats entice.
But Neurod shrieks, "He speaks! God speaks!" and they,
Panicked, listen gladly, watching madly,
Dumb with fear, our people dropping, stay,
Then broken, pray — "Please!" — following sadly.
    Wait. What *is* it in fire, ice, and thunder?
    Neurod leads while, stunned, I stare and wonder.

6

Death flows from birth, Deep Stream from which we draw
Our being, draw all change; we end, begin
Though sometimes desolate: the frozen jaw,
The somber eyes, and Neurod trembling, thin,
Pale, shrewd. He thinks, "Remove this cold from me!"
Then "Hmmm," he plots, "when I keep secrets, weaklings keep
Me warm if they believe that I can see
Those things to which they're blind. I'll probe, *grind* deep
Into their stress for 'Truths' they feel they need . . .
There is a pattern we must follow. Hear!
All who refuse bring us destruction. Heed!
Repeat past ways; from God's path do not veer."
    Past simplified and dire events foretold;
    A python's grip, religious fear takes hold.

7

High bounding Doe, astounding sleek-black Doe,
In trailing you we find a mountain pass.
How is it — lonely refugees — I know
Now where we'll go? I've dreamed this swaying grass,
These flower fields, these trees of fruit and bees
Through which fresh water turns. Fade, dreams of storm.
How is it, shining Doe? Intricacies
Unfathomable converge and take form;
With hope and joy we look down on lush lands —
Wild, strange — yet have we not been here before?
Immigrants in flight from Neurod: Join hands
With us for healing; let's resist Fear's roar.
    Discovery sparks a vow, our wish, our will:
    We'll find a way beyond our need to kill.

8

Inner tingling, full noon, mid-day, I am.
Sudden revelation, bamboo, I am.
Shaking leaves and branches clashing, I am.
Of us, bamboo (and you), we are, I am.
This new place, Arzen, fits us well: Peace-days!
We learn — through sitting quietly, patiently,
Aroused by breezes — of more tranquil ways
While feeling bamboo's striking unity
And lying with tame beasts upon their land,
The seed of beasts we once had killed to eat.
Alert from day to day, we understand
The needs of seeding grain; we set rows neat.
    Cool waters in our creeks run sweet and clear;
    Ripe fruit and nuts drop, spreading year by year.

9

Then Neurod reached us once again, somehow.
Cruel timing. Strangers hunger now for what we sow,
Fruit of our trees ("Get back!") and of our plow.
("Back!" Neurod never knows 'enough.') They go,
But not for long: It's clear they'll starve unless
Our reverence for life — for *lives* — takes hold.
Neurod insists that killing them is best . . .
No. Wait. If they will work with us . . . Be bold!
Neurod's restrained. We, risking, choose to share.
We walk, our children bearing bowls of grain,
Into the strangers' barren camp. "We spare
Ourselves in sparing you. We all will gain."
    Love makes us whole, and tears that teach us much.
    A reaching out — Yes! — fears are healed by touch.

10

Fast growing numbers hail the rising Sun:
"Accept our offer, this, our grateful song.
We'll join our race with yours and with you run
To speed your gift of light and warmth along,
For we're attentive to your faithful course.
We've planted seeds with neighbors many springs;
Both chant and dance accompany your force.
We need no walls or weapons, queens or kings.
Fair rhythms we have brought to harvesting
And soon our store of nuts and grain sustains
Us, frees us from dread winter wandering
When frantic hunters fight the freezing rains.
    We reach these lost ones, cheat war of its toll.
    In teaching them, we move toward our own goal."

11

Climbing children, swinging, laughing children,
Melody of carefree love returned. Bright-day!
That's the force that now inhabits Arzen
'Round our hearths, our homes. We work, my Love, gay,
Sparkling life with me, exhausted, joyful,
Safe with the food our communities yield
In our wide-spread fields. At sunset (awful
To Neurod, man of fear, spear, mask, and shield
Who groans that light may nevermore return)
We roll, my Love and I (beyond his cries),
Minds charmed by children's songs, flesh bathed in fern,
Invigorated flesh. Our high-tides rise,
    Wave after wave, above poor Neurod's snare.
    "Mother?" mournfully he moans. "Father? *Where*?"

12

Ach! Then it comes: feet pounding, sore on soil
So *thirsty* . . . Dance and drumming take new tones,
New tears. O desperate time, what use our toil
With spring so hot and dry that Neurod drones,
Through all our rites, of sins and sacrifice
That he would have us see as cause and cure.
By frenzy drained, our virtue turns to vice.
Chants, song, and dancing fail. ("Will we endure?")
We pray, we weep for food that never comes.
With scarcity old Neurod's power peaks
Till through our pure black doe his sharp spear hums
And blood he laps that from our doe's vein leaks.
    Survivors, we live on, but life seems vain.
    More gentle views are crushed in Neurod's reign.

13

For from the wanderers who had appeared,
Drear Neurod seized those weak enough to kill,
And as the land dried, by the sun's flames seared,
The tender died. "God's will we must fulfill."
Though springs of plenty soon returned, Neurod,
Obsessive, *clutched* his power, desperately:
"Beseech and tremble, fools, before our God,
Lest He repeat that past calamity!"
Thick walls went up. "Stop here, foul, impure race;
You may corrupt. We *own* the Great Beyond."
As shadows fell and apes fled — (Hide your face!) —
Pain, Fear, and Greed conspired: the ancient bond.
    We must be frank: They called it "sacrifice"
    But it was children who would pay the price.

14

Where are you, Courage? Rise up, Strength. I stand
In forest black and green, and long for sway
Of tree-tops yet am heavy on the land,
Alone, afraid, and sinking with the day.
My stomach turns and tightens round a surge
Of slow expanding waves, our inner seas;
Short breath, throat dry with memories of dirge
And hate . . . yet dove-songs draw me into trees
Where climbing, energized by hope, I gain new views
Of where we've been. Between the changing leaves
That mark our grieved farewell to summer's hues . . .
She's there, alive! Our bounding black doe weaves.
    Before we follow into crystal Time,
    Remember Arzen's victories sublime.

15

The ice came quickly, equalizing all.
Once more we fought and killed and grubbed to eat
While fleeing south in panic haste to stall
The onslaught, bitter, more than we could meet.
Though that year's cold seemed past all recollection,
Elders tell of strangest merriment:
"Some live and laugh for months without the sun,
Safe-housed in ice. Wolves teach them how to hunt."
And so it was and so it came to be
That running glaciers carried us awhile
And set the whole world trembling, seemingly
Oblivious to us, to all our guile.
    Rebirth takes shape between a breath and sigh.
    Our generations strive, exult, and die.

PART TWO: EARLY "CIVILIZATIONS"

16

Once hunger pain . . . How is it that I lie
Quite calmly on the sea today? Once cold;
Alone and cold . . . Now sun-warmed salt spray, fly!
I am these sails and sailors dark. Behold:
Drop anchor in a cove of Crete. Groves laid
With care and garden terraces slope near,
Anoint with perfumes our return, and shade
Safe-nursing mothers' breasts bared without fear,
For mother-warmth, life-bearing passions flow
To flute and harp, milk flowing. Small hands play
Across the pulsing flesh that babies know
Is theirs, soft heirs of seaweed and of clay.
    Wood from our land creaks, blending ship to dock.
    Our swaying walk the dark-eyed children mock.

17

We've traced our farms and mines to outcasts fled
Who feared change, parting, and the unknown sea
Less than the captive horde sick Neurod bled.
The sea repels, attracts. A yielding tree
Has roots. But this emancipated, deep,
Seductive cradle-rock: Who dared to think
Of crossing it? (Where *did* ancestor-dolphins sleep
That night they first crawled back?) We dare! Seas shrink.
Increasingly we reach lost land-locked tribes.
Wood creaking, yes, on wind-borne ships
We search and trade. Mark well, you honest scribes,
Our gains. And breathe, Soft Wind, through moistened lips.
    We learn of love, secure within our isle,
    And capture with our paint both tears and smile.

18

Sail back in time. Far roaming bands had burst
From arid hopelessness and found thirst solved
Along the Nile, this too a flowing breast
That swells to nourish. Egypt has evolved,
A chain of villages surviving . . . how?
What cost, what loss, to bind them tight?
Today we see a slew of workers plow
The river's gift, a bed for grain — seed flight! —
Tomorrow's bounty saved and put aside
For days when yet another human swarm
Will raise — in sweat, no choices, ease denied? —
Stones fit to soothe its leaders' fixed alarm.
    As pharaohs crave eternity to spend,
    Their pyramids defy both sand and wind.

19

Fine chiseled plans of those who rode the herds
Hid guilt (they hoped) through workers' lips cruel-sealed,
But artists still broke free in picture-words,
For morning-genius, fooling censors, had revealed
What masters and their priesthoods long concealed:
Brute power built on continuity.
Now forces from our primal roots may yield,
In time, our healthiest fruit, Community,
Where all will speak . . . in time. They have not passed,
The mysteries that moved us; have not died
Though pharaohs *fearing* Time continue their bombast:
"We shall endure forever!" Who has lied?
    "The Apes of Dawn," they pray, "adored the Sun,
    And hidden rites will with Him make us One."

20

Drawn dreaming up the Nile, I meet a girl . . .
Whoa! No! A *woman* sleek and shining black,
Unfettered, questioning. New paths unfurl
As in her hand I'm led (it seems) *far* back
Into old Africa, and we emerge
In Simrand, freedom land. My need, her need,
Converge (O Sweetness!), wild and sweet our urge
(Invisible to Pharoah's arms and greed),
Her world's peace, consummate, inviolate.
As once in Arzen here in Africa
(Millennia from our nightmare slave-ship fate),
We celebrate an innocent erotica.
    In peace and shade, we timeless lay.
    And, yes, in jungle trees the great apes play.

21

Searching on, through Arabia we crossed
In drifting sand, long restless nights by moon
And stars lit. Hot, those sands on which we tossed,
Exploring north, no paths, no guide from dune to dune.
"Tiamat, Mother, torn apart now whole:
Fertile are your plains! From mountains cool and still
Our Gods descended for their morning stroll
To feel, to be fresh water's sea-drawn will.
In Mesopotamia we're now seeds
Well-watered, yearning, thrusting up toward heat,
Forerunners of rich-fabled coming deeds,
A gate to singing and the dancer's beat."
    Love. Firm embraces with the rivers' might.
    Both past and future live in love's delight.

22

Harsh pressing of stiff stylus points in clay,
Hopes marked, fears masked . . . As gods to mountains seize,
Believers scan their ziggurats and pray.
Hallucinations mimic memories
Exploited soon by kings for power. Vain
Are steps of clay on high, thus comes decay:
Increasing shares of bright gold, fruit, and grain
Are stored away and bitter warriors say
That boys must also crack their neighbor's vault.
Most boys then bow unquestioning to Law
As warrior-laws compel our sons' assault:
Sick men seducing boys who bend in awe.
    Creativity from stubborn Chaos won
    Falls to Authority, peace-work undone.

23

But rare, clear moments, born of women, men . . .
You have them! Hold there, grow there, Steadfast Ones
Beyond despair; our time will come again.
Protect, preserve our fires; they glow like suns!
Conqueror, failure, hypnotizer, priest,
Set in your frightened struggle to acquire
Chimeric safety, crushing man and beast,
Of your self-praise and insolence we tire.
Who dares presume to show true people Truth?
Who breaks a fond embrace to teach of Love?
Who making war brings Peace to trusting youth?
Who claims, who prays that Glory waits above?
    Zarathustra, what will you someday say?
    Brave people persevere though priests hold sway.

24

Break loose! The road, the Way! We're climbing high
Back up the mountainsides down which we poured,
For we are free and reaching toward the sky,
Blue distance, home to all who've flown, who've soared.
Hurabo rallies brave but scattered bands
Of friends along their meadows and can see
A stage for new resistance. "Join hands
And minds," he pleads. "Who needs Security,
Sad slave by Order kept? Inhale the fields
Of lilies. Do they sow or reap? I'll not
Give birth to children and their pain; our shields
Are sieves. I'll feed the babies you begot.
    With goats we'll climb; we'll have no walled-up town.
    Possessing nothing, nothing drags us down."

25

Cross peaks to northern steppes; a lush plateau.
Hear now Hurabo's shaman, seen in dreams
Alive with mysteries, no need to know;
Winds — all past voices — fill her trees and streams:
"We are a pure, inexhaustible spring;
Our tribes have spread, and still spread, with the tide.
Once, flowing out from their primordial ring,
The keenest jungle progeny did ride
A wave of search, and, trusting, found this place,
Rich, fecund meadow where some procreate.
Observe our renaissance of challenge: Face
Yourselves; face turmoil, fear. It's not too late."
    Calm Bahdawils, our tribes are poised once more.
    Along your incantations we will soar:

26

"Source: nourishing Mother, long patient wait
For ripening Summer, enlightenment sought;
Come — finally! — earth-born Father, Autumn late,
For our decisive battles must be fought.
Arousing Thunder blast: hooves of the Horse
Announcing Wind and Water, siblings fierce
In persevering, flexible too, of course.
Then Fire's quick lightning: Day's perceptions pierce
The Mountain stillness, quiver on the Lake,
Indelible change settling with the Sun."
Swift Bahdawils, why do I tremble, shake,
As when on ice we, stumbling, had to run?
    "*I Ching* taps wells of primal caring;
    Draws from silent depths our calm *and* daring."

27

Sunrise! Bursting out from stagnant years,
We're on the move. Hail mystery! Hail chance!
No more the frigid sameness of some peers;
We're on the move. Hail ride and search and dance!
We cross wild rivers, lands, the new and strange,
Our Way; the goats and horses we have tamed
Are strong and, drawn beyond their natural range,
Astounding to the tribes past whom we've aimed.
An Old One dies; we turn with Bahdawils.
A girl gives birth; with Bahdawils we turn,
Imagination, perseverance, thrills
Reflected in her eyes: "Compassion learn."
    The lines of our experience grow deep.
    What Bahdawils sows, that we will reap.

28

Each night we bring to flames bright Fire
That, leaping, twirls from our ancestral wood.
Old tales mark goals to which we still aspire:
"In times of hunger, greatest cold, there stood
An ice-bridge entry to a hidden world
Where, following both birds and herds, our scouts
And wisest shamans dared, crossed, whirled
Into a land of dreams. Uncharted routes
Led past their sorrows, past Fear's steep abyss.
Vast continents spread beckoning; lands
Praised by ancient bards. Forgotten genesis?
Trust and Mutual Aid propelled the bands.
    Just so, our children grow and journey far
    With hope, with vision: sun and moon and star."

29

But never yet has progress been straightforward.
Always, it seems, we're called to be prepared
To face again our dark side, always hard,
For see this nightmare bark. (Who will be spared?)
Determined, pushing 'gainst the water's flow,
Propelled by twenty men chained fast to oars
And whipped across their naked backs (so slow,
It seems it can't be true), grim Neurod roars,
Voracious bird of prey, propped on the bow
Of the heavy craft, his spear reflecting
Certainty of pain with Arzen-peace now
Quite invisible. Neurod's expecting . . .
    What? I take my fears to Bahdawils.
    With her I find Hurabo and new ills.

30

"One Hammurabi, King of Babylon,
Swept through our mountains where he conquered all,"
Hurabo warns. "This man-lion claims he 'won.'
Round Sumer, Elam, and Akkad a wall
Of Law he's built, and safety from some threats.
But walls and safety bring no recompense
For freedom; dripping blood, the king begets
An endless thirst for vengeance. What's the sense
In this to us, raised not to sword or plow?
Some say 'Our Hammurabi doth mean well.'
What value is there in your pious vow
Of peace, Harsh One, for 'ours' and 'theirs' who fell?
    The slashing swords, the screams, the bloody night;
    What peaceful day can ever make war right?"

31

And now has newly come *this* mournful song
Of spring. Red buds and violet, green leaves
On blue sky, unifying blue . . . What wrong
Has quelled bird-song? Our apprehension weaves,
Alert (Come quick, Hurabo!), grieves and sighs
(Come, Bahdawils!), spring's promised growth destroyed
As we approach a place, a time, that dries
The wells of our enthusiasm. Void,
This bleakest and most sterile void, will shroud
The procreative season. We are drawn
And chilled by screams — by shrieks — upstream: a crowd,
Doomed prey of Neurod's pain, our bleakest dawn.
    Prepare, Hurabo, for another sight
    Of blood and might; prepare for Neurod's rite.

32

The living circle closes 'round a girl
And boy. Shrill reed. Drum throb. Discordant waves.
The young girl dances, doubt mixed with her whirl,
Fast, faster, frenzied crowd, while Neurod raves
Above them, shrill, above the curling girl
And circling boy who joins her, joining fear,
Their brief, pained, forced embrace, then caught, crowd swirl,
Crowd shout and rush and crush of stones . . . "Forbear!"
No chance. The sacrifice is swift, complete.
"This! Only this brings children," Neurod cries.
"*Rich*, our crops, our herds will grow. We'll eat.
Weed out the doubters, their agnostic lies."
    From dusk this burial mound throbbed alone.
    Now, Night, shroud pain here! Families rage and groan.

33

Still, bards preserve old images that traced
A once so potent, distant rumbling,
Time, the shifting land 'gainst which life braced;
Warring planets, stand-still sun, a crumbling
Of creation, Neurod's empire not exempt.
Never again forget: Uncertainty
Is King. Eternally our bed's unkempt,
And bards and artists tell of you and me;
Of epic woes, endurance, and travail;
Of deep collective memories that hurl
Us past the conscious sphere. We glide and sail
In dreams as our instinctive acts unfurl.
    Yes, Homers sing. And we find strength in this:
    Our infants recreate our tenderness.

PART THREE: GREECE

34

Fine rosy fingers, bright Homeric dawn
Alight within the eyes of Bahdawils.
Across Olympus trots a shining fawn,
Soon transformed — mirror-eyes of Bahdawils —
Into the strong, swift doe who led our way
To Arzen's hopes, that age of high delights
Till foiled by Neurod. Greece now feels the sway
Of Bahdawils renewed upon its heights.
We spin, dissolve. Opaque Olympian clouds
Enlivened by the sun ascend the peaks
Wherein we reassemble, treasured shrouds,
All set to fly. Through us a comet streaks.
    The mountain rocks beneath us move and melt.
    Dawn brings all shapes and shades that life has dealt.

35

"That which is bright rises twice: *I Ching*'s fire.
Enlight'ning, perpetuating brightness,
Illuminate the world. To this aspire."
Vast kingdoms rise and fall. *Ching* lightness
Passes, shimmering hot, from Bahdawils
To us. We faint, rebound, and sail above
Long centuries of strife: the pain, the ills
That plagued us. Shall we sing of hope and love?
"New energy! You're welcome at our feasts
To celebrate, at least, unwavering pursuit
Of clarity. We've driven back wild beasts
That on us preyed; tough crops have taken root."
    Can we hold and widely share our gain
    Then solve the pressing puzzles that remain?

36

A sea-bird circles, soaring high, our peak,
Cloud-gathering mountain top whereon stands
Zarathustra, laughing with all who seek.
He laughed newborn within his mother's hands,
And still this life he celebrates with laughter.
Sea-bird! Doe! Behold him, join him, free
While cloud-dissolving sunbursts break and stir!
Hear Zarathustra (and our memory):
"Leap light, awakening. Disperse the mist
And warm the tree that struggles forth from stone.
Though wearied by the brutal warrior's fist,
I've gathered strength, long having lived alone.
    Stay with me, watchful Doe, and, by and by,
    We'll high and fast as soaring sea-birds fly."

37

We are the sparks his dancing feet kick up;
We burn and twirl across the shining rocks.
The morn of Bahdawils has filled our cup
And high-noon's secret this our song unlocks:
"Our life is flaming water, liquid fire;
For us the deepest caverns are no trap.
We fill them, rushing on in our desire
To join rich midnights to fast-rising sap.
Earth's crucible supports our spiral spin.
Yes, Birth! (And Death . . .) Embrace this unique chance
While yielding clouds enfold our dreams within
Their arms, then we are yours, Immortal Dance."
    The far horizon's brightest red prevails
    'Round Zarathustra's dark'ning yellow trails.

38

"Howl, freezing Winds! And mountain Trees: *Defy*
While bending when you must. You're tireless
In your reach for the fleeing sun. No cry
For mercy, yours, nor flight from loneliness;
Atop the world stray lightning strikes and, struck,
You split and grow, indomitable still.
Earth shaking under planted feet, we're stuck
With tyrants, yet no tyrant breaks our will.
Come without hesitation, friends. Tempered
By the lightning bolt sloughed off, you're bold.
Ever stretching down and up, you've whimpered
Not at all; let's not now our strength withhold."
    Where are you forming, Steadfast Ones? Our age
    Must practice cooling the aggressors' rage.

39

"Everywhere we emerge, and nowhere; you
Are our emergence." Calm One, children die!
Why "calm," Siddhartha?   Is there nothing we should *do*?
"Tat tvam asi. Thou art that . . . and I.
Slow down. Turn inward and illusions pass.
A flame flares at our core: To give is All.
Forsake desire for equanimity.
Cling not to summer's joy; shrink not from fall.
To take-and-use or lend? To break or bend?
Drawn off, entranced by ripples, gentle waves,
We once were distant from our source, and Wind
To us was voiceless. Time no power saves.
    Shift, breathe, let go, turn in and see revealed
    Eternal images of all wounds healed."

40

Sky-lake-sea blue, endless, 'round our sea-bird,
Winging lofty, singing softly, flashing
White through endless blue; sunbursts on snow heard,
Melodies of sky-waves, sea-waves dashing . . .
Lightning eyes and easy breath: your thunderings,
Wise Bahdawils, alert. Let rest descend
On us, transfixed, and on our wonderings.
Yes, Sea-bird! Draw me closer still and blend
Untouched within the eagle's talons, white
And black, full-blended with our bounding doe
To fly again toward beckoning homes. Night
Approaches; light our way across the snow.
    Rise, Bahdawils, sharp moving silhouette
    Against the moon; the blazing sun has set.

41

Long-striding Zarathustra, peak to peak
Accomplished leaping, trail our sea-bird's flight
As we, along these long lost paths, will seek
To tunes created 'round our fires at night.
They open for us, meadows toward the sea
Below, the sea by mountain rivers fed.
Fine-tuned with you to river-melody,
I'll rest within your lotus lap my head,
Siddhartha, ferryman, until my eyes
Catch fire from yours at the rising sun. Before
Us, swim Doe! Swim the swiftest rivers. Rise
Then, Sisters, Brothers; see who thrives ashore.
    Their nightmare of the Minotaur jaw pales;
    Our riddle-solving Greeks unfurl their sails.

42

As sunlight spreads across the morning sea,
Sure, steady dominance, so swell Greek sails
With Wind that sings of our shared destiny
While Smoke, grey-messenger on shore, brings wails
From those whose sacrifice would slough off guilt:
"Forgive us, Gods, our Promethean theft.
Consume this blood; protect these ships we've built."
At sea, Telemachus drifts, bereft:
"Sire, dread Odysseus, never at a loss"
(Except for mercy; Hecuba's grieving
Tells as much in tears), "that rite across
On land seems sick, mere priests deceiving . . ."
    Theseus betrayed Ariadne, abused her key;
    Our labyrinth calls for loyalty.

43

"Brave children seek their parents, undeterred,
And, persevering, find them. So we too,
Telemachus, here on the sea — You've heard! —
Are bound by our most sacred bonds, *me, you*,
Yet sailing free. My son, look carefully:
As son and hope and heir, you're also my
Becoming . . . What's *that*? Speak you, Wind, to me
So sudden in my glory? You would try
My mettle? Yes, the grotesque price for you
That Agamemnon paid I now abhor:
His virgin child left, offered, given to
Appease you. And I . . . Polyxena . . . No more!
    Blow far from me the ghostly, ghastly bed
    Of sacrifice, and bring me life instead."

44

Bahdawils, helmswoman, speaks: "Odysseus,
First *face* Change, Change then will yield. But sleep
Now on the sea, soft-cradled, not by Zeus,
But by Penelope. Arise from deep
Within both son and husband, tossing there,
Strong, firm-supporting mother, lover. Sail
Unburdened, fresh, forgiving mind. The snare
Of Past brought into Now would have us fail.
Come, healthy pure exuberance of Fire
Allied with prescient Prometheus.
Rise and flare, not needing names, and we'll aspire
To understand our godliness. You. Us.
    But if you Greeks will not release your slaves,
      You'll never free yourselves. How Neurod raves!"

45

Flawed (of course) but searching, clinging to our rocky soil,
We know we must greet Change in its approaching hour.
We men gripped jealous rights to choose our toil
While women, patronized, long kept from power,
Found strength in unity. From Age to Age,
Embracing ("Hold to one another. Hold!"),
They saved our children from the hunters' rage.
Both girls and boys within a healthy fold
Find confidence through love and discipline;
Secure, then, they'll ignore both king and priest
And individuality they'll win:
Anarchist dreams and aims provide the yeast.
    The rapture of Dionysus no less
      Than cool Apollo's inward turn caress.

46

To Egypt, Solon sails in search of ways
To meet conflicting needs. He listens, looks,
For any signs of ancient wisdom's rays
Of hope, but what he's shown are dogma's books.
"You Greeks are children," mutters Egypt's priest
(This Neurod-clone afraid to be alone),
And Solon smiles: "As children not the least
Afraid explore, wide-eyed, and find their own
Paths, learning how to question everything,
Receptive to all doubts — and hesitations too —
Yes, Change we'll face and laughter we will bring.
But tell me, really, what you think is true."
    "We would remove the thorns of restlessness
    And doubt." (The doubt his hands and eyes confess?)

47

No labyrinth had bound us quite as tight
As Egypt's knots till cut by passion's will
When Nefertiti's spirit brought forth light
Within Akhenáten's heights and depths, and still
His joy resounds: "I would have all men feel
This love I feel; in her my God resides.
These pyramids of coldest stone would steal
The natural warmth of anyone." High tides
Rose up; gave way. Priests' power reappeared
With death, and Moses fleeing (Where's *Tikkun
Olam*?) tripped on a Patriarch who seared
And wrapped our curiosity in Fear's cocoon:
    "I'll have all power! Crush the ones who fail
    To bend to me!" Yahweh, jealous . . . (Questions pale.)

48

"But, Priest, see others on our childlike path.
From India ancient Vedas reach us, songs
Of forms emerging from the formless ("Wrath!"
Priests cry; "Beware God's wrath!"), song-search: 'Man longs
To know; knows not. Perhaps we'll comprehend,
Someday, those mysteries emerging ("Sight!
Priests have God's sight!") . . . or will we? Here *we* bend —
Must bend! — so rest, relax, in love's delight.'
Questions enriched Siddhartha's ground ("Death!
Dress for death.") to sprout those fertile seeds
From which emerged his clear and cool calm breath:
Siddhartha's growth past his desire's dense needs.
    Aroused by Shiva's graceful limbs, Old Priest,
       Let's leave your dirges for more music from the East."

49

Bells ring in China; gongs announce our song
Of struggle to survive: "In every land,
Birth's trauma, fragile infancy; we long
To be. Halt flood and famine. Fight, withstand
The downward pull. In Nature's temple be
Aware; force nothing, nothing leave undone,
For if there is a Way past misery
The balanced teardrops, Yin and Yang, show one."
A sage behind her great wall meditates,
Her mind an open field; to every breeze
She moves like flowers, reaching: "Know the states
I serve. Where are your true Authorities?"
    "Indian, Chinese poets, lovingly aware;
       As I head home, my Thales, have you dreams to share?"

50

"Save freedom, Solon. Freedom to inquire
And speak our minds." "Where, Thales, sprouts *your* joy?"
"In this: shade, groves, the sea, the leaping fire.
Each threat to freedom let our blaze destroy."
"What is most difficult?" "To know thyself."
"Ah, yes. And easiest?" "To give advice."
"From life well-lived, not just a dusty shelf,
Your son speaks out, Ionia. Entice
Him not to other tasks; the thoughtful walks,
The meditative hours pay well. From Crete
And ancient Mycenae *and* those with whom he talks
He learns. Now I must sail, my fate to meet.
    But, Thales, what is 'God'? This knot unbend."
    "Can you conceive of Beginning or End?"

51

"Home! Attica. Hard work and times to rest:
This marriage bears Strife's child, Discovery."
But, Attica, hear rumblings from the East. Digest
The threats of Cyrus which his minions see:
"Dawn breaks on Persia's day and ever" — "Yes!" —
"The sun will rise each morn on progeny.
Dreams tell me my responsive Queen will bless
Us with a son." "Fend off the enemy!"
"Humble mother rising, belly rising
With a boy who will confound the lie that
We could crumble through a sun expiring;
Vicious, untrue rumor." ". . . fears begat . . ."
    Greeks dream of moons eclipsed by children's blood,
    And ever suffer nightmares of The Flood.

52

What think you of Cyrus, Zarathustra?
Persian Cyrus, man of action, Vigor
Is his name. The slaves of Assyria
Hath he absorbed. Accustomed to war's rigor,
Patron though of gentle men, the dance
Is comfortable to him. And yet his son,
Protected Darius, has not a chance;
When his turn finally comes it's all been done,
The empire-building. Impotent, the lance
Of Darius; strong, the "allies" to *his* east.
Athens, avoid this hornets' nest. Enhance,
Build trust with Darius. Keep peace at least.
    Stop! Taunt him not . . . "My plotting foes you aid,"
    Protests the frightened king. "Feel now my blade."

53

Gory clash of steel again, again, and slash
Of flesh, and breaking bones; the tears, the screams
Of panic fear, the crush and bitter crash
And final going under: screams, shrill screams
At Marathon where frenzied boys and men
Of Greece and Persia stabbed and ripped and hacked
Each other, thinking they could win (again!)
Perspectives they *assumed* each other lacked.
Neither side could think, neither side could yield,
And so this time of horrors could not be denied.
Their children grieve now, wondering in that field:
"What moved our fathers here before they died?"
    In silence, dark, are wrapped both death and life.
    Rest, Beast of War; rest Spear and blunted Knife.

54

Rivers swum. Races run. For Greeks, peace won?
"Free" Greeks *talk* peace; it merely sleeps, The Beast.
Survivors lift their cups though it's begun:
The narrowed, proud, suspicious eyes. "Let's feast
And contemplate more victories." Men dream
Of prizes well beyond those once they sought.
In confident Athens (Spring's swelling stream),
They share, not nightmares, only *tales* of how they fought.
Aeschylus, soaring among mighty cliffs,
Trails questionings real enough to touch:
"Down should I hurl myself, free fall . . . ?" He lifts
Us skyward even as he writes of such.
    Another reads her play — "Attend, you men
    Of violence!" — hoping men will make amends:

55

"Power. Fire and wind and water, pliant,
Rise to my will and look to my control;
Athens votes me power. I, defiant
Fates, breathless as our destinies unroll,
Would have my people housed and safely fed.
Grim dreams and daylight fears, evaporate!"
"Warrior statesman, yes, we would be led
That we might with abandon celebrate
Survival and our gains. Hold tight the helm
And steer us through calm seas. You have our trust."
"Your trust, a child's last smile at sleep. Our realm
Is of unspoken doubts, uncertain thrust.
    But look. The sun falls brightly on our fields.
    Perhaps past danger to our power yields."

56

"We swim with dolphins, carefree; leap and play
In waves that wash across our gleaming backs.
We follow sheep along their flowered way
With shepherds and their dogs on beaten tracks.
Laugh, girls and boys! From mouth-to-mouth share grapes,
Then, after sunset, leave entangling vines
And climb those distant hills where love escapes
The grip of fear . . . for see: A full moon shines."
"Chained as Prometheus, I curse *this* 'rock':
My withering responsibility.
Clouds of concern for our tomorrows block
Night's festive light. Clear, Skies, for me to see."
    "By love refreshed, renewed, we dream: It seems
    We roll with dolphins, free, in soft moonbeams."

57

"Power, I must conjure you once more. Wait,
Neighbors of Athens! Empire will bear fruit
For you, but you must wait. It is our fate
That we must trade for food, thus does it suit
Our desperate need to rule . . . and you will lack
Nothing you need. Trust us to lead, to fit
A painless bond of unity. Hold back,
Impatient swords; we need you to submit!"
"What storm blows, stirs us from our sleep? Where sails
Our ship? What is this sound, this awesome wave?
Chilling remembrance of disastrous trails.
Our 'subjects' will not bend; *freedom* they crave."
    "Illusion. Delusion. I see — too late —
    The hate directed toward my laws, our State."

58

As thousands past the columned temples file,
Euripides, too, would have us hear:
"Old Zeus, if Zeus there be, what's with your guile?
By 'owning' slaves, men live in guilt and fear
For slavery puts us all in chains.
Trampled Melos! Can't you hear her cries?
Athens kills . . . for what? What justice now remains?
That peace of mind Greeks seek: Away it flies
As pregnant women men still dominate;
Brave women, children at their breasts. Rip, now,
Reweave Art's fabric, Greeks. Where's honor's gate?
Reconstitute yin/yang, male/female. Now!"
    Deaf, Athenians pounce on Syracuse;
    In salt mines, chained, they pay for their abuse.

59

Hey, chatting, strolling Socrates, we hear
Your teaching ways. Probe, caustic Socrates;
Extend sharp claws. Your syllogisms sear
Dogmatic nerves in our soft thinking. Ease
Not your grip, but think now, Gadfly-eagle:
Hear *us* when we point *you* toward the missing
Ones, the ones not at the banquet. Regal
Are your guests; their laughter veers toward hissing.
Missing are the progeny of Thersites;
They have no place, no voice at table.
"Voraciousness!" they yell. (They need not please.)
"Greek *freedom*? We'll expose *that* fable.
    Best cure for life, you say, is hemlock's tilt?
    Is life your bane, stern Socrates? Or guilt?"

60

And you! Does victory bless your master's death,
Torch-bearing, well-intentioned Plato? Caves
Receive your light and his; yet, still, your breath
Can only warm the willing. Madness raves
Unchecked, and when you, tiring of the fight,
Would over-simplify, paternally,
Lead, lull the gentle toward presuméd right,
You obfuscate our long-sought clarity.
Aristotle wraps heroic arms 'round
All the knowledge he can hold, and shares; yet
Lost — torch slipping from our hand — is the ground
That Reason's honest questions might beget.
    To Philip fratricidal Greece will fall
    And, falling, fail to pass the torch at all.

61

Philip of Macedon, you always get
Your way, but look to your son; his bravado
Is for you. Man of war, do more than pet
Your precious Alexander's head. The snow,
The burning sun will he, stripped bare, endure
For your approval. Ah, but death takes you.
Whom can your son please now? He will inure
The fallen Greeks to pain and lead them to
Assault his doubts. "Aristotle teaches
Me alone. The whole world my sole action
(See me, Father, racing, riding!) reaches."
Greek intuitions and a tireless run . . .
    "When I have fought and made that vast world mine
    I'll make it right. Bold warriors, we will shine."

62

Epicurus, to your cooling garden
Alexander comes. (To study? Or be seen?)
From the tragic stage of Neurod's Arzen
We have moved. Can you the conqueror wean?
"Breathe deeply, Alexander. Rest with me.
All search for Final Truth is meaningless.
Truth and beauty grow spontaneously
While intellect feels dimly their caress.
We show a way to live this life in peace,
A treasure not reserved for future men.
Through moderation, only, comes increase;
A garden's fruit and shade we all may win.
    Relax. The wars we once fought have been won.
    By enemies within are we undone."

63

Deaf, blind . . . Phalanx and cavalry are off to fight.
Alexander stops at Troy and, naked,
Streaks around Achilles' tomb. What a sight!
The Iliad and a dagger, naked,
Mate beneath his pillow. Innocent youth,
Best of friends; tears spring quickly to his eyes.
And, angry, sometimes thousands he (in truth)
Will massacre. "Defy me not!" The lies
About his generosity precede
The grim reality: another beast
Who kills when he feels right for it. Recede,
Romantic mist. "And, Master, *look* at least:
    You fight a lion then tremble at your cup."
    How can we help this pampered child grow up?

64

"See what I've suffered, Greece, on your behalf!
Suffered. Yes. Endured . . . and always won!
Here at the Indus sacrifice a calf
Then we'll go on . . ." "No, no. You're through, my son."
"Who *dares* tell me, 'No'? An old man, feet
In river, not unlike Diogenes."
"See here your limit, Alexander. Beat
Drums and trumpets blow; we hardly care. Please
Tell me what you think you're doing here."
"As Menelaus avenged his Helen's theft,
All unjust rulers I will strike with fear."
"Who strikes and who is struck? Who will be left?"
    "I . . ." Eyes opened, Alexander sees
    Siddhartha serene. Autumn sears the trees.

65

India and Greece: the sculptors seal a bond
With fertile silences; our inner world
Illuminates pursuit of light beyond
The nursery's tales. What challenge has been hurled,
O Restless Day? The great whales sail content
And sing blue harmony of sea and sky.
In tree and sky the apes swing indolent
And free; they swing and feel no need to fly.
O Restless Night, see Alexander's rage:
He slings his lance at Cleitus, killing one
Who saved his life. Remorse! Siddhartha, sage,
When will our fever cool? Is this age done?
    "Our voyage is long and though the sea is dark,
    Fear not, Brave Ones, as once more we embark."

PART FOUR:
ROME, JOSHUA OF NAZARETH, THE "DARK AGES"

66

"Rush to me, day of mortal pain; this night
And our immortal longings are not spared
Yet love remains. Hold fast to courage. Light
Will ever sparkle from the love we shared
For we were undeterred by worldly strife.
Attentive, O so clearly we could hear
(We all *may* hear) vibes soaring past this life
As we transcended pain and fear.
Such arrogance, these men astride their State;
Sparks fly from crosses, from our crucified,
Igniting questions that infuriate.
See Rome's perplexity; she thinks we've died.
    In shedding life, we see what life was worth.
    Rome stays behind, imprisoned on bare earth."

67

"I dream men press me with their wants and needs
And, as I struggle to be fair with all,
Tight (tighter!) grows the choking cord that leads
Me toward my grave. Awakening, I stall;
I would sleep on, oblivious to threats
(Where have I failed? Where is my son?), and die,
But I must rise and pay this new day's debts.
'Marcus Aurelius!' our people cry
While thinking me the most secure of men,
Yet Commodus, my son, I cannot trust . . .
I long to trust. What if we fail? What then?
The laurel wreaths fall when and where they must.
    These men called Christians, what is it *they* seek?
    Who was this Jesus Christ of whom they speak?"

68

He was a man for all that we could tell.
He sought, through tenderness, to overcome
Men jealous of his powers, those who yell
For crucifixion of the bothersome.
"Love ye one another." Plain, his words burned,
Shamed our Neurods. Hold, Youth! Hold to love and doubt
For, straight from cross to Boss, the man was turned
Into "God's Son." (Your effigy carved out
Too, Siddhartha, hangs in Neurod's lair.)
A neutered Christ emerged, insipid, pale,
A mirror image of themselves; a snare
To catch our new-born birds, wings wet and frail
    Like Isaac on his father's altar plate.
    Marcus Aurelius, the hour is late.

69

"Indeed, but slowly, slowly do we learn
Through our mistakes. Rome, once so fragile, stern . . .
In warrior myths of proud Troy's fall and burn,
We hear dire warnings. Listen, you who yearn
For justice, opportunity (Hope's pull):
Rome struggled through its infancy. 'The more
One longs for peace, the more vulnerable
One becomes,' cried a frightened king. War's roar
Was constant as Rome won the highest ground
Then from Carthage took the African sea,
But now I understand what Terence found:
'Nothing human is alien to me.'
    Justice for all, *protected* by our state;
    We'll persevere. Perhaps it's not too late.

70

"Remember that the Gracchi brothers spoke
For Rome *and* for those lands that shared her peace;
Their idealistic aim was not to soak
The world for Roman comforts, nor to fleece
Our lambs then let them suffer in the cold.
Today let's try new paths to unity.
Long-ripe female power is ready to unfold
Beyond our strong-man insecurity.
But, yes, it is *so* late. Come, you who care;
Step forth again, step *quickly* while you can
For gates are closing fast . . . Where are you? *Where?*"
Closed! We'll have to leave — for now — what we began.
    (Survival will depend on rest, Provence. Rest well.
    We'll waken to your Troubadour's clear bell.)

71

". . . again across our farms the hunters run.
The Roman rich own land they never plow,
Take slaves to fight their fights and, yes, my son
Commodus sleeps with gladiators now.
I'll sit along the Danube for awhile
As legion fires burn low. Cold river-grey
As must to Hadrian have seemed the Nile
That swept belovéd Antinoüs away,
Let's seek life's fresh pastels. Vitality, leap past
Despair at pain, at fear, and flare once more.
Across the Danube virile tribes rush fast
Upon us; soon into our midst they'll pour.
    The vigor of these tribes; the energy . . .
    Come, friends. Let's face the changes Rome must see."

72

"Enchanted mariners sailing the night,
Bedouin riding waves of heat and sand:
Like these we have been tamed, transformed by bright
Celestial harmonies above our land.
Protecting our providers, fruitful herds
Up on the steppes, we've tuned to ebb and flow,
But now we're pressed by swarming northern hordes
Too hard; across the Danube we must go.
I am Hurabo, true to Bahdawils.
Repulsed by Neurod, risking the abyss,
We've rediscovered mountain-childhood thrills
While on the move; sloughed off paralysis.
    Rome, trust our instincts. Give us, too, our due.
    Commodus, open to our song's fresh hue:

73

"Slowly, all through the night, the dipper wings
Out from the pole star which remains in place
While — hear! — a nightingale's clear love-call rings
From tree to tree 'round us, eternal race
As vivid as the dashing of our herds
Into the lakes and creeks. A shepherd's joy
Is in fresh water, sun, cool grass, and words
That pass from lovers, lip to lip. Annoy
Us not with tales of what the future holds.
This kiss, a breath of scented air and hair,
Our softness, wetness: Life from love unfolds.
A kid rests in the wolf's abandoned lair.
    Join hands for moments fully lived and felt,
    Aurelius, and Rome's mistrust will melt."

74

"Our history, Hurabo, bends to you.
What pledge or law could discipline your flow?
You are a force no empire can subdue;
The fates assign me futile tasks, I know.
We cannot take your hands though I *do see*
The contrast that my words and deeds present.
Sad Commodus; sad, bitter progeny!
What chance have you, have we? The times have sent
Us roles: a king, perhaps, who's lost his touch,
And his poor fool on whom the curtain fell
Too late. But silence, peace. I've talked too much.
An emperor should at least die well."
    Hot or cold, dry or damp, Death strips us bare.
    Our wise Aurelius is gone. Beware.

75

Mistrust has melted not and Chaos reigns;
Rome, once so fragile, stern . . . The pendulum
Swings wild and fierce. On masters' wrists, now, chains
Of misery cut deep. Harsh morn has come
For those who slept secure in their belief
That Change would not reach them. The edifice
Of classic style rots and a sterile thief
Dines on aristocrats whose orgies this
Resembles. Rebel-heirs of Spartacus
Stride starved but free, while infertility
Saps energies from sinking Rome. "With us,"
Hurabo hopeful pleads, "find unity!
    If joined in courage and goodwill, perhaps
    We'll reignite flames Rome allowed to lapse."

76

Shit! Let me waken from this gruesome dream
For surely it cannot be real. These cries
Must be an echo from the past; a scream
From childhood. Wake, Hurabo! Wake and rise,
Alert. Hammurabi, Alexander,
Commodus . . . now *Constantine*? (Too late. Too late!]
He's purring platitudes (Gross slander!),
Prancing on his stallion, off to celebrate
(Of all things) The Nativity (!) while Saxons, *crucified*,
Adorn his route to church where "Sacred Truth"
(*The* Truth) is dished out to the stupefied,
Choking their pride, their will to search, their youth.
    Where we had crossed the Danube full of hope,
    We're trapped between an emperor and pope.

77

Darkest night's long test: our nightmare of despair.
I know, Hurabo. You are weary too,
Gripped by the horror, stark and bare:
Merest illusion seems our faith, untrue
Our bright belief, that someday all would reach
Your love and high ideals. Again appears
Our cycle's deepest trench, and we teach . . .
What? In power, 'Christians' prey on weakness, fears.
To live or die? To stay or fly? I feel
Death's steady pull though Life's voice summons: "Live!"
I long to shatter and I long to heal.
If I withdraw, will I myself forgive?
    The vicious and the dull, the cruel and tame:
    Can I at least choose not to play their game?

78

Away! Out from peopled places, I'll let
Summer's selfless bounty feed me, yet
It's looming, always: Winter's daunting threat.
Anxiety the Killer must be met,
Yet . . . do I hurt too much to care? I need
Community's embrace, but feel I've nothing
To give back. A soul that's gone to seed,
Can I survive with no song left to sing?
What's waiting in this dismal forest spot?
Weakness? Shame? The impotence I dread?
No. Wait. Steep yawning, fright'ning depths are not
Unknown to us. Look on the trail ahead.
    She runs, our doe, strong bounding, black and brave.
    I cannot let her down. There's something we might save.

79

Zarathustra's sea-bird dives before me,
Dives, cuts, climbs into a pool of blue
Which, shining, crowns the tallest forest tree;
She finds the path through which our wise doe flew.
Creek pebbles roll downstream in wind and sun,
Whispering rhythms of discovery:
"Swift, strong, and clean, here birth and death are One.
Come feel and find your own entelechy."
A monastery looms before our eyes:
Stone walls which bear stark signs of many storms.
A weathered door cracks, opens to what lies
Within: a circle, shadows, fire-lit forms.
    With Bahdawils here dancers celebrate
    That fear-bred Hate we may obliterate:

80

"Welcome home, soft Sea-bird. Perched on our wall
While resting for awhile, you're no less free.
From Attica came a Clarion Call
Whose echoes vibrate for eternity.
Consider Grecian search that once moved us.
We will preserve that mighty catalyst
For rebel minds and hearts," she vows "and thus
Surviving, transmit what is simplest.
Our doe, curled safe in blanketing shade,
Is not asleep; all past winds live upon
The current breeze, and though she will evade
A tempest here, she's always set to run.
    Let yourself go, breathe, dance . . . then join our chant.
    Communal seeds of radiant Hope we'll plant."

81

My mind is racing to avoid itself;
A swarm of high emotions makes demands.
But intimations dawn of one true Self.
Can I trust myself on shifting sands?
I learn to chant; my tension bends and cracks.
I breathe, breathe free, as stress is letting go;
Obsessive worries lose their grip. "Relax,"
Sings Bahdawils, "and feel your Stillness flow."
The monastery door is closing, see?
Hear sounds of clapping and of opening tombs
As Hate dissolves, turns to Serenity:
The calm of mothers' breasts and of their wombs.
    Auummmm mani padme. Peace, our breath, our One.
    Secluded flowers growing toward the sun.

PART FIVE: A RENAISSANCE

82

Winter mystery, dark force locked in ice,
Silent prisoner of Time (still as I),
Dream-borne, shadow deep and still, entice
Me, wakening, to wonder as I lie
Attentive through deep breaths and inner gaze
Which, joined, rule a world of Motion's grace
Whose subtle powers challenge me to blaze
New paths of curiosity. Embrace
Our moment, swift Imagination; pierce
The veil that hides me from myself. Aware
In this seductive silence, calm but fierce
Be mindful also of the hunter's snare.
    The captive in the ice had seemed immense
    As densest night intensified suspense.

83

And now a spot on our horizon grows
With the rising sun, and grows. A cry,
Faint, penetrates the morning sky. She flows
Toward us, our sea-bird singing, winging by
To land, stretched, spreading 'cross the icy form.
What journey have you made to meet this morn?
With what strength did you pass the winter storm?
Where is the flock within which you were born?
The hunter's misfired arrow splits the ice
And from the captive force a fresh bud leaps,
Unfolds, seeks light. Released from winter's vice,
Seize opportunities while winter sleeps.
    Come out, brave Doe. Eat, drink, and stretch; take wing.
    Rejuvenated, help us greet the spring.

84

We climb, pulled forth by eagerness and dreams,
Pulled through familiar hesitations, lost
In the thrill of climbing. Harsh, the past screams,
Impotent to break this spell, night's bright frost
Melting in the early sun. Though mountains'
Heights accost all confidence, our brave doe
Leads us toward a cliff where springs, like fountains,
Burst — break free — from crisp, still-frozen snow.
Great Morning, cresting over sleep's domain,
Ignite our resting place; this hope surround.
Light caves where bears — dark primal fears — have lain.
At overwhelming dawn . . . what is this sound?
    Remembrance, flashing through me, sudden, clear:
    I've heard this song before. I have been here.

85

Is there reality within my trance?
Across receptive earth Semeuse swings high,
Her seeds in flight throughout her work and dance,
Life-bearing arc of arm against the sky.
Semeuse, one with her fecund, moist plateau,
Feet sturdy, warm on liberating soil,
Back muscles rippling, strong to sow
The rhythms of our future, love and toil.
Semeuse, you're sending me (mysterious Source!)
A touch of Beauty's power — and dreams of more:
Firm strokes, arousing tenderness, life-force
Soft whispering: "The time has come to soar."
    A yearning seed takes hold in me, Semeuse:
    A throbbing need you've planted . . . Muse? Come, Muse!

86

The vision fades in morning shades. Where once
Ice formed — inflexible — clean water flows
And Doubt, companion to Exuberance.
Monastic grace expands, explodes, and knows
Libidinal passion for the world,
For conflict, creeds and freed minds clashing, Fire
To test endurance, and a flag unfurled:
Our challenges and hopes. Semeuse, inspire
The Violent to control their blinding wrath
And to reflect; inspire the Sensitive
To be as brave as they are true. Our path
Must lead through thorns and flowers; strive, *forgive*!
    I'm drawn away, Semeuse, Fire in my Heart!
    So open wide, my Searching Mind, and make a start.

87

"For such a mind awakening, your troubadour
Will sing and, singing, bring our hopes to life:
The Rule of Love. You've tasted it before,
This force that transforms histories of strife:
'Mist, Muse, and Memory, rise from your spring
To me, impatient devotee . . . we wait.
Come breathe clean-flowered air where bird-songs ring,
Sharp, fair. Why do you hide down there? It's late.
For laughing girls we long, for one our love
Grows strong, to her we raise our song, secure.
Surely you understand, a dove above
Rich land, we, lifted by her hand, endure.
    You often call to us from deep in sleep.
    Rise, Muse, to sing! We'll let our old fires leap.'"

88

"Hail, Friends. A most receptive muse you've stalked.
Andalusia saw my light restored;
Where Trajan and Hadrian crawled then walked,
I held the power to sheathe stern Allah's sword.
In earth's harshest crucible, first cousin
To the frozen polar sea, Hamāsah
(Our Enthusiasm) grew. Bedouin
Poets raced past Allah, past Jehovah,
Star-struck, finding melodies to fly
With their hypnotic desert tunes; a brew
To quench religious dogmatisms dry
As sand, and in Provence I'll reach for you."
    Yes, I awaken celebrating change;
    Semeuse has opened this expanding range.

89

War-obsessed Muslim, Christian, Jew: Imbibe
Not Certainty but Search. Explore! Recede,
Brute creed. Hamāsah (Fortitude), inscribe
In stone, not blood, this answer to our need:
"A desert dream of jungle peace we'll learn.
In Cordova three cultures join hands.
The healing power of the inward turn;
The tolerance a free mind understands."
In Roman order we had long forgot
The fertile anarchy of youthful awe.
In Andalusia, at last Hate's knot
Was disentangled; some who looked now saw:
    In spite of Pain, Fear, Greed — sad Trinity —
    War need *not* last for all Eternity.

90

In Provence, free-thinkers also learned to share;
Shared love, shared hope as well as bread. Here each
From within found "saviors," laying bare
Their loves and hopes, uncensored. Pristine beach,
A landing dock, inspired Hurabo's home,
And Bahdawils'; constructions built of mind
And spirit, rule of heart replacing Rome
With this: "Recover sight when we are blind."
But still those men addicted to tamed love
Of *their* god . . . never quietly do they fade
Though caught, exposed in New Love's day. Above
You, Church and barons plot; they draw their blade.
    We praise free spirits, brave to sound the call.
    Your story will remain, and Love. That's all.

91

"Foul heresy!" (Poor threatened pope.) "God's work
Be done!" (The barons drool for land.) "Doubt turns
My Faithful from The Way!" (Berserk,
The frightened pope.) Free-thinkers plead, *"Love yearns
To find and then protect a righteous throne . . ."*
Blunt knives (and minds) cut Reason short: "He'll know!
Omniscient God will recognize His own.
Our fold we must keep pure and clean as snow."
"God's pity! My child bleeds!" At Beziers
And Carcassonne crusaders heed their Papa's call:
"Kill all, I say! God knows His own! Then pray
That our supremacy God will install.
    Ah, that is better . . . better," sighs the pope.
    "*Now* we can breathe in Christian peace, I hope."

92

Still in Provence agnostics dare to reach.
Though all tough questions we find cast away,
We'll try again — again! — to learn. (*Then* teach?)
Through cool, sustaining woods we'll make our way,
A course clear-marked by instinct's subtle print
Down forest passageways to light and shrines
Deep, deeper under trees and hopes unbent.
Though faint, Semeuse, a dark still center shines.
Here lay Iseult; adoring Tristan came.
Here Lancelot was one with Guinevere.
And dazzled Parzival, he without blame,
He too searched here and felt his Grail was near.
    But ever-distant, our elusive goal.
    My fire burns low; dream-visions, dark and cold:

93

Night thunder rising from a herd in flight.
Strong creatures lead; they storm across the plain
While toward the rear, with those too young to fight
And with the old, the weak, the sick I strain.
A predator is closing in, his eye
On me. He has the body of a beast
But, cruel, his face is all-too-human: sly,
Voracious, mauled by Greed. On me he'll feast
For I'm fast-losing now the will to run.
I smile a forced, brief, grotesque smile of pain
In darkness, knowing that the farce is done:
Attachment to this life seems morbid, vain.
    And yet I tremble, struggle on, and shake.
    Where am I? Who am I? I must awake!

94

The center point revolves, appears unchanged;
Though herd-sounds fade, Fear stays and I'm alone.
Guarding a gate, a stranger; he seems deranged,
But past him, in a town of wood and stone,
Is safety here behind a higher wall
Within an order carved and held in place?
No, no. We run and fall and rise and fall;
We strive but sense no "winning" of this race.
(Come! Come, long-sought Consistency!) Peace turns
To desperation, calm to storm. But here
Find rest when troubadours pass through; one learns
(At times) in towns like Mantua to steer.
    And then, one day perhaps our hopes come true.
    Safe day, great ape, will we swing freely too?

95

Meanwhile, what games were played! One Richard, *Coeur De Lion*, Keeper of The Faith, marched east;
Against Saladin — also "faithful," sure —
Dick sported chivalrous. Unnatural beast:
No lion has killed in sport. The game's absurd,
Obscene and worse. While cowards kill from fear,
Still needing to control the herd, The Word
("Our God is One!" "No, Three!"), watch "Truth" appear:
Black Death. This killer scales our highest walls
With ease, and, indiscriminate as men
Who did "God's work" at Beziers, he crawls
Indifferent to distinctions: Sinless? Sin?
    "I will be saved!" the dying cry, "I'll live!"
    While — deaf — the Savage Killer shifts his sieve.

96

Come, gyre turn. Mind-learn. Spiral free. I see
A river and Siddhartha's shaded place,
Time's chasm vastness bridged by memory
Here, midway in the wood: the Buddha's face.
"Mihiragula, Mahmud, Khan. Despite
Delusion's tricks, the cooling river flows
To soothe our wounds, to wash the deathly rite
Away. Refreshed, a Golden Flower grows.
 . . . riverrun . . . sleep, poet of the long fast,
Day done, night to come. Float on our river,
Forested. Drift – calm – back toward the sea, past
Watery root to parent stock. Deliver
    Him, Great Mother. Wrap him in your soft wave.
    Sleep, my son, and sail. Futile, past fears rave."

97

"Who are you?" I don't know . . . "Hmmm. True, it seems.
Courageous. Life lived free of answers."
Semeuse? Seed-sower! I have searched in dreams . . .
"And mine. We've reached a time for dancers."
Red in a "New World" sunset, Wanshee drums,
Our black doe at his side, and seems to make
The mangrove glow around his tribe. He hums,
New wells spring forth, and dancing children take
Their cue as Wanshee sings: "Warm Mother Moon,
Light playing on the ice we crossed, caress
These voyagers; they will ride your glaciers soon.
Mark generations of courageousness!
    Yes, Searching One, Semeuse shines for *your* dance.
    Rise to our drums; our swift doe's joy enhance."

98

A fresh day's sun on young green leaves, and blue,
Both sea and sky, crack through our long sleep. Land.
Your hand! I waken to the warmth of you,
The sweetness of your body on the sand,
Semeuse. To move, to breathe with you at last,
Expanding, stretching, free in your embrace . . .
"Receive, Sweet Love, our tremor and this blast
Of soothing passion, nature's healing grace,
Presentiment of birth we all will know."
Arousing ocean breeze. Firm touch, moist heat,
Volcanic surge that melted primal snow,
Ah! Ah, Semeuse. With you I am complete.
    The ecstasy of rise and fall: All this,
    Surpassing simple as we yield to bliss.

99

Wanshee sings: "Hail, Dawn! Hail, Magic, ripe for you,
Semeuse. We'll hear you now, Child of the Sun."
"The power of the firm, and yielding, too.
Both yin, both yang, we are each other, One,
Wanshee and Bahdawils. As empathy
Joins the land and sea, all is at last laid bare.
Each night we fly, receptive, trusting, free,
And morning's dreams we with the dreamed-ones share.
Wild tribes around us moan and would forget,
Suppress remembrance of the cold. They chase
And kill, make war, long to forget, and yet
When mirrors of our Old Ones' eyes they face,
    They're awed. Then darkest dreams to us they bring,
    And to a glimpse of saving Love they'll cling."

100

"Reflecting light from Bahdawils, we give
Her life for, yes, from 'cross the roughest sea
Have travelers come to me and said, 'To live,
Wanshee, I yearn. Give me the power to be.'
Recall the dance of Zarathustra. More:
Siddhartha's stillness dance. Recall the peace
Hurabo's people knew. Arzen restore.
Thrive, living long before the ice, then cease.
Become the sun, the moistened land. Bow! Bow
To bold Semeuse, her out-flung hand, her cheeks
Flushed, blood-rushed, seeds in flight, and be here now.
Inhale. You are the power your courage seeks.
    Just ride the wind, ride down the running stream.
    Relax. You are a dream within a dream."

101

We dive into a tropic sea with whales,
Glide, rise with them up through the polar freeze;
A woman stands alone, tuned to the gales,
To whales and wolves, their icy symphonies.
She stands erect, a silent glacier's tip;
We spin and fall, out toward her waiting nest,
Loose, safe in falling. Here we end this trip
And lie within her arms, at peace, at rest.
"Semeuse, most precious are your gems — ripe seeds —
For us. And yours, her firm supporting Sail,
Your daring to be fertile. Our world's needs
Call out, Semeuse. May you and he prevail.
    Follow your sea-bird; fly beyond the herd."
    We rise again to follow you, Swift Bird!

102

Misguided quest for what is "real?" The plan
Of Bahdawils? Your touch, Semeuse? Desire?
This lovely Tuscan town? Look at the man
Among his books, enchanted, one on fire.
"I am Petrarch. Your troubadours have taught
Me, too. In Avignon we sang the night
Of Europe's sleep away then, climbing, sought
A mountain's grace and ancient words' delight.
Heracleitus, buried, is reborn;
And Epicurus, Plato on my shelf
Debate. The arrogance of princes shorn,
We search for wisdom: 'Look first to yourself!' "
    Rich tones reflecting from a perfect dome
    The youthful hopes of Athens and of Rome.

103

Renaissance! Michelangelo roars
Above dull Creed and Greed. Genius, arise:
"Yearning forms were trapped in marble cores
(Old threats, Savonarola, that you recognize!);
Captives cold as once in ice. Eternal forms,
Potentialities, again you're free
From 'neath oppressive weight; your latent storms
Flash, *thunder* through my hands toward liberty."
Pope Julius would have your genius chained
Beside his tomb, great Michelangelo,
But mighty prisoners you've already freed. They've gained,
We've gained, and let's make sure the world will know.
    Savonarola fought against the tide
    Of our awakening. We would not hide.

104

Hurabo? Why the crowd in Rome today?
"A heretic will burn." A heretic?
Four centuries have passed since Beziers!
"It is the same, the same Rule of the Sick."
Impossible. Pale, frightened children wait,
Appalled, in parents' arms. This cannot be!
Hurabo chained? Compassion foiled? "Too late.
Here comes a 'Pope' – Neurod's insanity."
"Speak, Giordano Bruno. Come on. Speak!"
"I doubt all absolutes. I doubt your way.
Eight prisoned years of pain, yet must I seek . . ."
"Quick! Tie the tongue that dares. On with the play."
    Enough! You fiends! This is our Hope that burns.
    To arms! Look. Phoenix from the fire returns.

105

The aristocracy of Church and State
Would be the center of the universe,
So Galileo, risking Bruno's fate,
Must also speak the doubt he feels, withstand the curse,
For he conceives the universe a sphere
Whose center point is everywhere, unbound,
Evolving free: "What are the views they fear?"
And music! Nature's harmonies resound;
From Montaigne's tower to Shakespeare's London stage
We mark the progress of heroic lives:
"And readiness is all." It seems an age
Of Reason and of Reckoning arrives.
    Deep in his own eyes, Rembrandt finds our scope.
    He reconciles Reality with Hope.

106

But *still* our 'Rulers' dance their minuet
While, still, Hurabo seeks new strength: "Blind fools
And deaf, you dance a dance of death! Your pet,
Beribboned, flies from 'neath your feet, you fools;
She feels the storm that gathers, rising fast.
You dragged a genius boy from court to court
To play blindfolded. Hear the storm's first blast:
Mature, his music echoes your lame sport.
The sky grows dark behind your children's swings
In Goya's paint; wind stirs your powdered wigs
As injured Figaro forgiveness sings:
'Take care! It's *your grave* that your coldness digs . . .'"
    No way. The outrage stored in suffering
    Breaks loose in Don Juan's mocking laugh and sting.

107

"God, have mercy! Please!" "No! Revolution!
Talking, waiting done. On to the Bastille!
Crush the Cruel, release the True." For one
Night's dream, *Equality!*, and masses reel
In dizzy spontaneity. Such strength
(Dread strength) this day: great feat-surpassing-feat's
Exhilaration! "Go to any length
To rid the world of tyrants. Now we'll eat!
Come, who will lead? We're not afraid to bleed."
The "masses," meaning well, rise, surge, and swell.
"We're not afraid. Show us the way. Our need
Is simple: bread and liberty. Just tell . . ."
    "Yes, come (my simpletons)," foul Neurod grins.
    "I'll show you. Follow me. The first one wins."

108

No, Neurod! You, your clique, your gang of friends,
The greedy, selfish ones, the ones who could
Not make you out: Here you will end. "*It* ends.
But I, Neurod, will never die. Look. Good.
The glint, the falling gleam of Guillotine;
I am reborn . . . as Robespierre! Revenge!
Serve pain for pain." Through priest and libertine,
Through patriot and king, the blade, the hinge
That creaked some last complaint at closing, drips
Well-oiled with blood, and blood spilled frees more lust
For blood. All Europe shakes. The trembling lips
Of rulers mutter, "Crush France into dust."
    Hurabo staggers, trying to be fair:
    "Napoleon, help us these cruel days to bear."

109

Betrayed. Hurabo views our field of strife:
"You helped yourself to riches and a crown,
O Bonaparte. The boy who gave his life
For you, who trusted you . . . his hopes went down
And jealous Chaos, like the Sea, reclaimed
His own. Neurod. Again we're in your snare;
Gripped by your cycle — Pain, Fear, Greed — we're maimed.
You've tricked our children not to think or care.
Prepare – someone! – a rooster for Asclepius ***
For I'll accept his Cure . . ." Hurabo's end
Observe; a path long-trod he clears for us.
The dagger plunge, the final lunge, attend.
    Unwrap base funeral drums; mute wailing horns.
    Hurabo dies with flowers and with thorns.

110

Yet fire and cannon rumbles could not dry
Our sea of inner sound — Beethoven's might! —
Nor mar the landscape of deaf Goya's eye.
We'll not resort to either fight or flight.
Not yet. Our challenge still: to love and strive.
And when a peasant whips a struggling horse —
"The tender eyes, Karamazov! I dive
Into this madness, drown!" — beyond remorse
At fading dreams of that which should have been,
Nietzsche is drawn out toward a lonely shore,
And, going under, still he'd bring us in:
"Do not forsake the hero at your core."
   Quick, Love! Rush toward the drums our "Indians" beat.
   Fidelio lives past this day's defeat.

*** Author's note re verse #109: Asclepius in ancient Greek philosophy was the god of healing. Thus the tradition that, when healed of a disease, a person would show appreciation by sacrificing a rooster to the god.

When Socrates was put on trial for the capital crime of corrupting young people of Athens, it's apparent that the philosopher could have saved himself but chose not to do so. Instead, according to his pupil Plato, Socrates calmly, willingly took the drink of hemlock and, as death neared, made one last request of his friend Crito, who was in attendance: "Crito, we ought to offer a cock to Asclepius. See to it, and don't forget."

Classical scholar and poet Friedrich Nietzsche interpreted this as indicating that Socrates saw life itself as a "disease" which only Death has the power to heal.

EPILOGUE: OUR "MODERN AGE"

111

Semeuse has sailed Siddhartha's proven realm
As, receptive to Fire, her courage rose.
A Satyagraha comes to share her helm;
This man whom elder women by consensus chose.
He – Wanshee – recollects: "When soldiers came
With greed to claw and chew a 'New World,' Fear
Repeated 'Old World' crimes; again its name
Was Ignorance, insipid, cruel. But hear,
Red folk, long-fortified with wrath, with 'fight':
We've known a Way! And heir of Simrand Blacks –
Of death-ship agonies, chained day and night –
Harriet Tubman added drums and backs,
    Unbreakable. Yes, kindness *might* prevail
    And Auschwitz/Hiroshima tactics fail."

112

New knowledge can not be suppressed. Einstein saw
Into the atom and the universe:
Our double edge. We must no longer draw
A line that marks off Us from Them. Reverse
The ancient challenge; deal with *our own* fear:
Who has the love to touch and heal Neurod?
He holds a button where was once a spear.
Nagasaki, Fukushima . . . whose God,
Plutonium? "Ahimsa," Gandhi pleads,
Non-violence on the scales with Faust's desire.
After all these efforts, need we fall to 'needs'
Of Neurods plunging *under* ice and fire?
    Our force that was deep-frozen has returned;
    Can we save and heal with powers we have learned?

113

"Poor paranoids! Fear threatens to control us all,"
Sings Bahdawils, embracing yet again the day.
"Fear's power holds such energy in thrall!
But life-on-ice recall: We've known the Arctic Way.
Certainties of outgrown creeds will crash, fall,
Crushed by a quantum jump in consciousness,
No clue its coming, sudden, here for all,
Ideas exploding, neither more nor less
Than evolution, Arzen's revolution
Realized." "I wish I'd stayed," Hurabo
Comes with Wind, his voice in rustling leaves, "shunned
Death, Semeuse, your progeny to know.
    Global warming; polar melting. Youth, arise!
    And don't be fooled again by leaders' lies."

114

Semeuse waits, clear and cool; this dawn will bleed.
Breathing patiently, she waits upon a surge
Of life; fulfillment of her yearning seed.
She'll let go, giving of herself, the urge
To live and let live overcoming pain.
Soon vibrant life will flow. She'll breathe and push.
She'll reassure: "Come forth, our precious child. Both rain
And sun await you. Love can help you. Shhhhhh."
Life's wondrous voyage! Semeuse brings us reprieve.
Our baby breathes, reflects Fire's healing light
As, gathered round, we celebrate, receive,
Pass on the spark of Bahdawils, the might:
    "We love but do not own the seeds we sow,
    For all love is in part a letting go."

115

"Rest now your weary heads, mother and child.
Rest for your first night under moonlit sky,
Rest covered by a quilt of stars, soft, mild,
And gentle in their touch. I, Bahdawils, must die.
From sea to land to tree we rose for you
While never knowing what would come for you . . .
So crawl, walk, run in wonderment anew
Here near the End of Time. Run and renew.
Our Innocence, Semeuse, lies at your breast.
This guardian of all our hopes will grow
To find and know forgiveness through our quest.
Sleep well, my children. Dream. My passing know.
    The door is opened wide from whence we came;
    Our first songs and our last, they are the same."

116

A silence absolute and stillness be.
We are at first a pulse beat, nothing more,
Immersed, drawn up (Old Ocean Mystery),
No pleasure, pain, reluctance as we soar,
Free, through ascending beats, slowly at first,
Then faster. Faster! Shall we risk? Yes, *dare*
Though wondering: "Who are we? Will we burst
From this acceleration?" Well, look there.
Rise up! See life as from a limb above:
Soft-dappled light illuminates a child
At peace among the trees with all who love
To climb, to swing; with all who're reconciled.
    Leap down. Run unafraid, a doe at play.
    Run faster with your friends. You'll find your way.

"THE VOICE OF SCRIPT"

REPLICATION AND PARAPHRASE*
A 1983 commentary on *Receptive to Fire*
By Elwin "Ed" H. Powell
    Professor of Sociology
    State University of New York, Buffalo

"Dedicated to John Schwinarski, Buffalo philosopher, upon whose mind I have 'symbiosed' for years."

Note: During the thirty years since Dr. Powell's research and ruminations for his "Voice of Script," anthropological discoveries have, I think, not significantly altered the glorious sweep of his views on evolution. So, except for bringing the lines he quoted from *Receptive to Fire* into conformity with this latest version, I have left his work as it was in 1983. — B Wardlaw

A. **We Made Ourselves Through Mind:
   From Idle Curiosity to Passionate Inquiry.
   (Prehistory, Circa 5,000,000 to 12,000 B.C.)**

By 'reading' nature and developing an ever more ingenious 'script' the primates prevailed, man emerged. To read is to guess, foretell, estimate.[1] By scanning the environment and 'decoding' signs of coming danger we learned to live successfully in trees, "past all need to kill" (*Receptive to Fire*, Stanza 1, Line 10). And because tree-life was full of existential challenge, the brain grew — a 30-pound monkey has a brain as large as a 78-ton dinosaur.

With the big brain came "remembrance mixed with power to forget" (*Fire* 1, 13). Unlike the dinosaur, we moved beyond instinct, concocted a new script for survival. *A script is simply a plan of action.* Around five million years (myr) ago we left the trees — perhaps driven out, maybe drawn out, "mesmerized into pursuit of distant tones?" (*Fire* 2, 7) The brain has its own hunger, a thirst for new data to process. Human evolution is propelled by both a push and a pull.

Ground life called for new solidarity; not the trees but one another was our main protection.[2] Thus emerged the primate band, itself a kind of social mind: each member sends and receives information to and from all others and the group responds to threat as a single collective unit. One for All, All for One! Altruism is a survival mechanism: it is the unwritten script of the primate family.[3]

Around 4 myr the family bifurcated: the ape-script stabilized, the man-script evolved. The first known man-ape, Australopithicus Africanus, had a cranial capacity of just over 400 cubic centimeters (cc) — roughly the equivalent of a chimpanzee. The ape-apes we will call Alphas; the man-apes the Omegas. The Alphas were happy, well-adjusted forest vegetarians. The Omegas were misfits and derelicts who "went to the dogs," became scavengers. The Omegas ingratiated themselves with jackals and hyenas and got cut in on the food-take, learned food sharing, became meat-eaters and eventually hunters. "By constant association with and observation of large carnivore tactics," says Simpson, "true hunting strategies emerged . . ."[4]

With this new script came explosive growth of mind and brain. The typical Alpha Ape lives in a territory of 15 to 20 square miles, while a wolf-pack covers 500 to 1500 suare miles as did our Alpha Ape. Activity stimulates brain growth — the principle applies even to rats.[5] As scavenger-hunter the Omega brain enlarged over 4 myr to 1000-2000 cc. The chimps are still at 400 cc.[6]

Hunting, says Laughlin, puts "motion and direction into the diagram of man's morphology . . . places a premium on inventiveness and problem solving . . . and imposes a real penalty for failure."[7] The hunting complex consists of four behavioral components — programming the child; scanning for information; stalking and pursuit of game; immobilization and retrieval of the game. The hunter becomes a 'scientist', a seeker after knowledge. The vegetarian Alpha Ape can often get by with idle curiosity; the Omegas acquired a passionate need to know.

Out of hunting came the fundaments of science (1) precise observation, and (2) propositional language, i.e.: theorizing. The hunter 'reads' the action of the prey from perception of the tracks — "If track . . . then deer" — an hypothesis derived from a general theory of the script of the deer; knowledge gleaned from observation and passed down over generations. "In trailing you we find a mountain pass," reads a line from *Fire* (7, 2). We observed animals, learned from them. Not by conquest but assimilation did our knowledge grow. As we moved out of temperate zones 700,000 years ago, the males were the scouts and trail makers, thus became the leaders of groups on the move from camp to camp. Only as a hunting society were the higher latitudes accessible to us, says Carl Sauer.[8]

From following the herds came new social knowledge, sympathetic insight. If life with the carnivores made us ferocious (Robert Ardrey's killer-ape thesis), life with the hoofed animals gave us compassion, imparted patience, even wisdom to the human species (*Fire* 7, 1-2, 13-14):

> High bounding Doe, astounding sleek-black Doe,
> In trailing you we find a mountain pass. . . .
>> Discovery sparks a vow, our wish, our will:
>> We'll find a way beyond our need to kill.

Man identifies with the deer, incorporates the deer script into his own repertoire of response. In our earliest burial sites (70,000 B.C.), deer antlers were interred with the deceased, and our earliest necklaces and pendants (50,000 B.C.) were made of reindeer teeth.[9] There is a Paleolithic cave-drawing of a man with stag antlers; perhaps by assimilating into animal-hood, man was becoming a god in his own imagination. When Alexander the Great had himself declared a god, he put on stag antlers to symbolize this divinity.[10] By putting on the antlers of a stag, man was learning to behave *as if* he were a deer, learning propositional language. Learning *if*-ness.

Mind begins in imitation: we copy the action of the other and then re-do it *as if* it were our own; first we replicate, then we paraphrase. Man becomes the deer, absorbs the deer script and acts it out in dance and ceremony, paraphrasing it in his gesture. So, too, do we assimilate the character of our human ancestors by taking over the role of the other (George Mead's phrase) into our own consciousness. Thus we learn to speak the words of others as if they were our own: *Saying is Always Resaying*. Such is the paradigm of every intellectual activity from deer-herding to poetry-writing.

In *Receptive to Fire*, B Wardlaw replicates whole libraries of information and tells a story of civilization in 116 sonnets, a paraphrase without parallel in our time. Here is history as song. Jasperson says the human race learned to sing before we learned to talk, and poetry precedes prose as written communication.[11]

Speech developed as a means of giving voice to the script we are writing with our lives, came as a means of 'narratizing' the inner world of image and emotion. As our mental capacities expanded through the hunting-herding experience, information accumulated which required organization as knowledge. And as Tanner and Zihlman write:

> As hominids became more and more enchanted and troubled by dream images, a need for symbols to define and order meaning emerged. Such symbols could be used to communicate not only remembrances of dreams but to share memories of what was seen or done during the day with others after returning to camp. . . . As speech developed, perhaps it was less essential for teaching motor skills associated with food gathering . . . than for constructing beliefs and rituals to deal with death, for telling stories and relating dreams, musing about the past, and proposing tomorrow's activities.[12]

Speech developed as an aid to story telling. *The story stores information.* Note the linguistic connections. To store means to lay-away, accumulate . . . to place or leave in a location (as a warehouse, library or computer memory) for preservation or later use. The word story initially meant history, an account of incidents or events . . . a legend (*Webster's Intercollegiate*, 1974, p. 1147).

Man was telling stories before he learned to speak. Objects were used to store information, memories. The *object trouvé* — a special gem, feather, a piece of coral — communicates in some way beyond the usual, and as Paul Shepard says:

> When such objects are incorporated into a human construction, such as a necklace, chain . . . an arrangement of pieces of driftwood, or the drawings of the eyes of an owl on a head-shaped rock, their significance is raised to a new level, as though the finder had completed the fragment of a sentence. . . . *Objects trouvé,* which uniquely relate man to nature, are worn, traded, scrutinized, imitated, and treasured. Neanderthal man apparently collected such objects. Australian aborigines keep a collection of such stones for religious purposes. . . . They stand in a special relation to human sensory and perceptual systems,

intermediate between human productions and the given world of natural objects. They anticipate human productions, not just as products but art forms. Therefore the *object trouvé* is a substitute (or natural) work of art . . . linking the given and the created.[13]

The *object trouvé* is a memory aid, a memento: it is used to replicate the past, to recall significant events. Out of the process comes the sentence, the completed thought. Speaking is the act of making sentences, not simply uttering sounds. Man learned to think by manipulating objects — and then reflecting on his actions. In building an *object trouvé* man is writing — the process requires editing: what to keep, what to discard. He is arranging objects which have meaning to him, and that meaning is derived from the response of others in his community, his social network.

Full speech, vocal speech, came only with the ripening of our contemplative nature; when we could abstract ourselves from immediate and threatening pressure and reflect on the meaning of existence. It came, not in the heat of day but in the cool of evening. It must have come in a place like Arzen of *Receptive to Fire* (*Fire* 8, 5-14):

> This new place, Arzen, fits us well: Peace-days!
> We learn — through sitting quietly, patiently,
> Aroused by breezes — of more tranquil ways
> While feeling bamboo's striking unity
> And lying with tame beasts upon their land,
> The seed of beasts we once had killed to eat.
> Alert from day to day, we understand
> The needs of seeding grain; we set rows neat.
> > Cool waters in our creeks run sweet and clear;
> > Ripe fruit and nuts drop, spreading year by year.

However, this paradise of *Receptive to Fire* is temporary. Soon it is threatened by hungry ones from the hills. The people and the new invaders join hands, make friends. Neurod, the leader, thinks killing them is best.

Neurod foments strife in order to solidify people behind his own rule. Neurod, the would-be god-king, is the voice of authority. In earlier times, simpler days of the Alpha Ape, the oligarch is never questioned: What the leader commands, the troop does. But in the course of human evolution a Self emerges and the authority of society weakens. Much human history henceforth pivots around the question, whom to obey — the inner voice of reason and conscience, or the outer voice of power and coercion (*Fire* 5, 1-14):

> Entranced, one moment, by the face, my face
> (Yet yours) aglimmer in a pond of ice,
> An image, clear dimensions fit to trace
> Our journey. Birth's red morn to death's night splice.
> Transparent, candid ice . . . turn . . . Crash! The gift
> Of rare serenity is split, thick ice
> By lightning torn, our image torn and rift,
> And I'm adrift . . . Such cowardly retreats entice.
> But Neurod shrieks, "He speaks! God speaks!" and they,
> Panicked, listen gladly, watching madly,
> Dumb with fear, our people dropping, stay,
> Then broken, pray — "Please!" — following sadly.
>   Wait. What *is* it in fire, ice, and thunder?
>   Neurod leads while, stunned, I stare and wonder.

Neurod of course thinks he knows the one true script — there is a pattern we must follow and those who refuse will bring us to ruin. Repeat your ways: replicate the past. To re-do the known is always soothing — such is the principle of ritual. In good times we put up with Neurod, let him rant and rave. But our nonchalance he cannot abide: he organizes a hunt, provokes fear — a deep unconscious script dictates we turn to the father in times of fear. Most people comply.

Then comes the ice, "equalizing all" (*Fire* 15, 1). The last thrust of the Ice Age was around 20,000 B.C. The Mediterranean became a virtual arctic, with average temperatures of –10° Fahrenheit for nine months of the year. "Once more we fought and killed and grubbed to eat . . ." (*Fire* 15, 2). But we survived . . . and retained the skills learned in these millions of years of evolutionary experience. By 10,000 B.C. we were writing new and different scripts . . .

B. **Derivation of New Script:
    The Voice of Early Civilization.
    (Circa 14,000 to 4,000 B.C.)**

The human script has been in process of formation for 5 myr — but Barkow would say 15 myr. The script is partially genetic, partially cultural. Basic dictates of directives of the script — a kind of grammar, if you will — may be inborn: Barkow postulates a system of 'protonorms' present even in our arboreal ancestor Ramapithecus at 15 myr. These protonorms direct the child to look to the mother and the dominant male for orientation; the protonorms create the 'attention structure' out of which consciousness evolves. The attention structure gives cohesion to the primate community: unless we were pre-programmed to read the gestures of each other and derive therefrom the appropriate meaning, the band would fall apart.

    Gesture 'bespeaks' script. Mammals learn to 'read the script of the other — the mouse understands the motions and motives of the cat, and even the tame house-cat carries in its genes rudiments of the skill of mouse-hunting. Animal life goes on in a "conversation of gestures" — to use George Mead's phrase.

    For man the vocal gesture — speech — takes on pre-eminence in the last 40,000 years. Gesture, transmuted into sound became voice, the main integrator of the human community. Those who mastered the strategy of verbal command rose to the top of the dominance hierarchy: not the physically strongest but the best speaker became the leader. And best meant getting others to obey, to hear. "To hear is a kind of obedience," says Julian Jaynes; "the word obey comes from the Latin *obedire*, which is a composite of *ob* + *audire*, to hear facing someone."[14] How then does the leader insure obedience? By convincing others he speaks with the voice of god (*Fire 6, 6-12*):

> "Hmmm," [Neurod] plots, "when I keep secrets, weaklings keep
> Me warm if they believe that I can see

> Those things to which they're blind. I'll probe, *grind* deep
> Into their stress for 'Truths' they feel they need . . .
> *There is a pattern we must follow. Hear!*
> *All who refuse bring us destruction. Heed!*
> *Repeat past ways; from God's path do not veer."*

The brain is already working overtime — hallucinating, hearing voices: it only remains for Neurod to step in and define the meaning of the message.

Around 10,000 B.C. the first human settlements — villages, towns — appear, quite possibly the creation of women, of what Elizabeth Gould Davis in *The First Sex*[15] calls a 'gynocracy.' As the last of the Paleolithic hunters followed the big game into the oblivion of the northern wilderness, the women, left behind, cultivated the arts of civilization — weaving, pottery making, the domestication of animals, the planting and harvesting of crops — such is the thesis of Davis' remarkable work. Ongoing excavations at Catal Huyut in Anatolia (modern Turkey) are tending to confirm that in the earliest cities there was a balance of power between women and men; that Mother Goddesses were ascendant; and that peace prevailed — without benefit of walls. By 6,000 to 5,000 B.C. gynocratic culture had spread across Europe and to Malta and Crete, indicating the development of seafaring technology.

Who are these people who settled Europe and the Mediterranean basin in the Neolithic (8,000 to 4,000 B.C.)? Deviants, they seem to be the ones who have given up the hunter-script and moved into a new life-style (*Fire* 17, 1-8):

> We've traced our farms and mines to outcasts fled
> Who feared change, parting, and the unknown sea
> Less than the captive horde sick Neurod bled.
> The sea repels, attracts. A yielding tree
> Has roots. But this emancipated, deep,
> Seductive cradle-rock — who dared to think

> Of crossing it? (Where *did* ancestor-dolphins sleep
> That night they first crawled back?) We dare! Seas shrink.

Sailors are reaching the land-locked tribes (*Fire* 17, 10-14):

> . . . Mark well, you honest scribes,
> Our gains. And breathe, Soft Wind, through moistened lips.
> > We learn of love, secure within our isle,
> > And capture with our paint both tears and smile.

And there is activity stirring in Northern Africa, around Egypt (*Fire* 18, 1-3):

> Sail back in time. Far roaming bands had burst
> From arid hopelessness and found thirst solved
> Along the Nile . . .

Villages grow and cluster along the Nile — here is the beginning of the transition from clan to state. People do not live in scattered huts but gather together behind solid walls of the village, over which flies the ensign of the clan. People work the river and fields by day, return to the village where they have defense and mutual aid, presided over by a council, an oligarchy of influential elders. These villagers are the people who built interminable networks of irrigation canals, banked the river, drove out the wild animals, built the flint and ceramic industries, learned to cast copper and gold. "To this prodigious labour we may assign a period of at least 1,500 years (before 3,500 B.C.)," write Moret and Davy. In addition, they say:

> The result of these centuries of discipline is civilization visible for the first time on earth. By the end of the fourth millennium in Egypt writing was assuming definite shape with combined phonetic and ideographic signs, thus increasing a hundred-fold the resources of the old picture writing. Thenceforth memories of events could be preserved in other ways than by oral tradition; acquired experience was handed down; history and political tradition were created.[16]

The Neolithic was a time of building: it seems to have spread from the north of Europe to the south. Strange megaliths went up in England at Stonehenge and Avebury. Often the building seems to have been an end in itself: Stonehenge they worked on for 1,500 years — perhaps the building provided employment for males who were once absorbed by the hunting role. And the pyramids and ziggurats . . . were they built by slaves, by true-believers serving god, or simply by people hanging out together, enjoying each others' company? The assembly circle at Avebury could accommodate 250,000 people, presumably come together to pay homage to the Mother Goddess: a kind of early Be-In, a pre-historic Woodstock.

A collective enthusiasm may have inspired the building, but very soon it was taken over by the god-kings (*Fire* 22, 1-5):

> Harsh pressing of stiff stylus points in clay,
> Hopes marked, fears masked . . . As gods to mountains seize,
> Believers scan their ziggurats and pray.
> Hallucinations mimic memories
> Exploited soon by kings for power.

The building was done by the people, the product was seized by the state: control passes into the hands of an elite and (*Fire* 22, 10-11) "boys must crack their neighbor's vault" and "bow unquestioning to Law" (*Fire* 22, 13-14):

> Creativity from stubborn Chaos won
> Falls to Authority, peace-work undone.

What then to do? The system is now too vast to overthrow. But this new state where "priests hold sway" (*Fire* 23, 14) is no place for a free man. The only option is to split: go to the hills, or to another city.

Hurabo — a recurring script throughout *Receptive to Fire* — joins a band of resistants in the mountains, returns to a tribal life (*Fire* 24, 13-14):

> "With goats we'll climb; we'll have no walled-up town.
> Possessing nothing, nothing drags us down."

Farther north is Bahdawils, Siberian shamaness, voice of primordial culture (*Fire* 25, 5-10):

> "We are a pure, inexhaustible spring;
> Our tribes have spread, and still spread, with the tide.
> Once, flowing out from their primordial ring,
> The keenest jungle progeny did ride
> A wave of search, and, trusting, found this place,
> Rich, fecund meadow where some procreate . . ."

Following their herds, tribes even cross an Aleutian ice-bridge and are "whirled into a land of dreams" (*Fire* 28, 7) — the unpeopled continents of North and South America. The script of Bahdawils also flows southward into Persia where it is absorbed and reformulated by Zoroaster. Two words compress the wisdom of Bahdawils: "Compassion learn . . ." (*Fire* 27, 12)

But in the south the spirit of Neurod soars, a "voracious bird of prey" (*Fire* 29, 9). Hammurabi has swept through the mountains, conquered all, erected walls and well-meaning laws. Still he can never erase the soul-stain of conquest: "What peaceful day can ever make war right?" (*Fire* 30, 14)

Early kingdoms — Sumer, Elam, Akkad — were absorbed by Babylon, which itself dissolved in the extraordinary tumult of the 2nd millennium B.C. Religion as the "hallucinated voice of god" — the "bicameral voice" Julian Jaynes calls it — was the main cohesive force of these pre-literate civilizations. A shared god-script enabled bands to cohere into tribes, tribes into city-states. People assembled in the city for sacred ceremony.[17] The nucleus of the city was the shrine which became a temple; in houses, a separate room was set aside for the family god. A priest told the people what god said, and the message was always the same: follow the script. But in the upheaval of the time the voice of god was scrambled, the gods gave contradictory instructions. In the Paleolithic hunting society, god was a co-equal with man; but in the city, god moved toward omnipotence as man shrank toward impotence, subservience, and obedience. The totemic religion of the clan gave way to the 'humanized' religion of the state, presided over by a god-king.

Probably the godless, the outcast, the deviant had the best chance of survival. Jaynes mentions that a whole island civilization sank in an earthquake.[18]

> Warring planets, stand-still sun, a crumbling
> Of creation, Neurod's empire not exempt.
> Never again forget: Uncertainty
> Is King. Eternally our bed's unkempt.
>
> (*Fire* 33, 4-7)

C. **Exploring Alternative Script:
    Emergence of Consciousness in Greece and India.
    (Circa 1,250 B.C. to 24 A.D.)**

When a word is written down it takes on a new and different voice: consciousness grows out of the effort to imagine the sound of silent marks.

"Into human history around 3,000 B.C.," writes Julian Jaynes, "comes a curious and very remarkable practice. It is the transmutation of speech into little marks on stone or clay or papyrus (or pages) so that speech can be seen rather than just heard, and seen by anybody, not just those within earshot at the time." [19]

Writing brings sociality into solitude, nurtures the inner freedom of subjectivity. Our word liberty derives from the Latin for book: libre. With writing, commands give way to queries . . . and it begins in Greece where the gods come down from Olympus and man becomes the measure of all things. Now comes (*Fire* 34, 1) the "bright Homeric dawn." And at *Fire* 35, 11-14:

> . . . "We've driven back wild beasts
> That on us preyed; tough crops have taken root."
> > Can we hold and widely share our gain
> > Then solve the pressing puzzles that remain?

A new delight in the wonders of existence entered the ancient world (*Fire* 36, 3-5):

> Zarathustra, laughing with all who seek.
> He laughed newborn within his mother's hands,
> And still this life he celebrates with laughter.

And psychedelic luxuriation in contradiction (*Fire* 37, 1-14):

> We are the sparks his dancing feet kick up;
> We burn and twirl across the shining rocks.
> The morn of Bahdawils has filled our cup
> And high-noon's secret this our song unlocks:
> "Our life is flaming water, liquid fire;
> For us the deepest caverns are no trap.
> We fill them, rushing on in our desire
> To join rich midnights to fast-rising sap.
> Earth's crucible supports our spiral spin.
> Yes, Birth! (And Death . . .) Embrace this unique chance
> While yielding clouds enfold our dreams within
> Their arms, then we are yours, Immortal Dance."
> > The far horizon's brightest red prevails
> > 'Round Zarathustra's dark'ning yellow trails.

And sensual pleasure in contemplated script (*Fire* 38, 1-6):

> "Howl, freezing Winds! And mountain Trees: *Defy*
> While bending when you must. You're tireless
> In your reach for the fleeing sun. No cry
> For mercy, yours, nor flight from loneliness;
> Atop the world stray lightning strikes and, struck,
> You split and grow, indomitable still.

Thus with Zarathustra out of Persia (*Fire* 41, 5-6 & 14):

> They open for us, meadows toward the sea
> Below, the sea by mountain rivers fed. . . .
> [Where] riddle-solving Greeks unfurl their sails.

Meanwhile, Siddhartha, also a spiritual descendant of Bahdawils, plays out the inner script of subjectivity, of the awareness of awareness

Receptive to Fire — 91

(Jaynes' definition). The natural world is illusion — and the creation of our craving. Forsake desire and discover joy. "To give is All." (*Fire* 39, 6):

> Shift, breathe, let go, turn in and see revealed
> Eternal images of all wounds healed."
>
> (*Fire* 39, 13-14)

Siddhartha comes out of Vedantic India. For 1,000 years the Vedas had been kept alive as "oral script," committed to memory and chanted by the priesthood (*Fire* 48, 2-3):

> From India ancient Vedas reach us, songs
> Of forms emerging from the formless . . .

Holy men could recite — replicate — 'books' of Vedic scripture verbatim, and quite naturally resisted the idea of translating their sacred lore into written form where the uninitiated could gain access to it. As the Vedas were transcribed on paper, religion began to leave the temples and permeate the streets.

So, too, with the *Iliad* and *Odyssey* in Greece which once were "devoutly chanted to vast audiences . . . by bards or *aoidoi*."[20] In the *Iliad* man is an executive carrying out the commands of the god: "Not I was the cause of this act, but Zeus" — hence Jaynes' notion of the bicameral mind: one chamber, mere receiver of instructions from the deity, sends the message to the other chamber for execution. The events of the *Iliad* take place around 1,250 B.C.; those of the *Odyssey* some 250 years later: Homer is not a single person but one of the *aoidoi* — perhaps the first to publish (around 1,000 B.C.). But by the time of the *Odyssey* the self — the "I" — has emerged as actor. And it is at this time that writing is becoming widespread in the ancient world. Over 2,600 years ago, Greek soldiers on expedition in Egypt left written accounts of their lives carved in cliffs. Ramsey says that these show a much higher level of literacy and of civilization than anything left by the Christian crusaders 1,700 years later.[21] [Paper had been in full use in Egypt by the 4th millennium — says

Ramsey — and according to Herodotus was in ordinary use in Greece by the 5th century B.C.] Ancient writing, however, was not produced for private and isolated consumption, like the modern novel; rather it provided text around which dialogue grew: the written word was a thing to be talked about.

And above all it was talk — dialogue, argumentation — which was the glory of Greece. The Greeks seem to have 'talked it over' then decided to resist the massive totalitarian army of Xerxes: It is said that a mere handful of rational men held off the Persian hordes at Thermopylae. The Greek city-states united for defensive war, and afterwards came a great fluorescence of creativity. People — merchants, farmers, artisans — are seeking a way to rule themselves.

The Greek consciousness, nurtured on Homeric tales of individual heroism, sustained by dialogue and drama, embodies the full contradiction of human existence: enslaving freedom, chaotic order, satiated longing. Always (*Fire* 54, 5-6), "Men dream of prizes well beyond those once they sought."

> Aeschylus, soaring among mighty cliffs,
> Trails questionings real enough to touch:
> "Down should I hurl myself, free fall . . . ?" He lifts
> Us skyward even as he writes of such.
>
> (*Fire* 54, 9-12)

Why then did Greece go under? Greek Reason — Logic — Logos — was undone by the long Peloponnesian Wars. The Greeks lost capacity for sensible debate and calm deliberation. "The meaning of words had no longer the same relation to things," wrote Thucydides in 426 B.C. "The lover of violence was always trusted and his opponent suspected. . . . Revenge was dearer than self-preservation." War between cities, within cities . . . state war, class war.

And still deeper even than war is the master-slave script. "By enemies within are we undone" (*Fire* 62, 14). The best and brightest of the Greeks seem not to comprehend the lethal poison of hypocrisy:

preaching freedom, the Greeks live off slavery. They cannot hear Euripides' impassioned plea (*Fire* 58, 4-5):

> By 'owning' slaves, men live in guilt and fear
> For slavery puts us all in chains.

Even Plato (*Fire* 60, 6-8):

> Would over-simplify, paternally,
> Lead, lull the gentle toward presuméd right,
> [And] obfuscate our long-sought clarity.

Losing touch with the primitive reality of equality, the Greeks forgot how to "take the role of the other" (*Fire* 50, 5-6):

> "What is most difficult?" "To know thyself."
> "Ah, yes. And easiest?" "To give advice."

Gradually the Greek world slides into ruin. After the exhaustion of the Peloponnesian Wars, Philip of Macedon steps in, brings order and Alexander, the world conqueror who is self-conquered. At the Indus, Alexander is stopped by Siddhartha who asks him to explain himself. "All unjust rulers I will strike with fear!" Alexander says (*Fire* 64, 11). Siddhartha asks, "Who strikes and who is struck?" (*Fire* 64, 12). This Alexander cannot answer and he comes apart, while Siddhartha is left serene (*Fire* 65, 5-8):

> . . . The great whales sail content
> And sing blue harmony of sea and sky.
> In tree and sky the apes swing indolent
> And free; they swing and feel no need to fly.

D. **Logos Unhinged:**
    Out of Roman Ruins, the Christian Script.
    (Circa 24 to 500 A.D.)

By the year 24 A.D. — the year of the execution of Titus Curtisius — Force (not Reason, not Logos) rules the ancient world (*Fire* 69, 8-9).[22]

> . . . War's roar
> Was constant as Rome won the highest ground.

The people had no voice in the political community — the popular assemblies were wiped out during the class-war, the 'revolution' which brought Augustus to power. "The individual has become a unit unto himself," writes Karl Kautsky, "and no longer possessed the feeling that his activity would endure in the state."[23]
But gods were plentiful, and even manufactured by the Roman Senate which declared Augustus and most of his successors to be divine. "To be the son of God was a portion of a redeemer," Kautsky notes, "whether he was a Caesar or a street preacher."[24] Today, the interesting questions are not theological but sociological: Why did the street preachers win?

Generous indifference to the gods of others was a Roman virtue. Only years later does Marcus Aurelius ask who are these men called Christians . . . and this Jesus Christ (*Fire* 68, 1-6):

> He was a man for all that we could tell.
> He sought, through tenderness, to overcome
> Men jealous of his powers, those who yell
> For crucifixion of the bothersome.
> "Love ye one another." Plain, his words burned,
> Shamed our Neurods. . . .

Yet Christianity catches hold and lives while Rome withers, dies. Why? (*Fire* 13, 12):

> Pain, Fear, and Greed conspired . . .

And the root of the pain and fear? Is it not isolation, aloneness? Money, possessions can give a kind of influence over events, a voice in an *ersatz* community . . . hence the greed.

But, as an answer to the pain and fear, early Christians provided a real community. What Christ himself may have been, or said, no one can know — none of the Gospels were written earlier than 63 A.D. However, a functioning network of congregations existed before their scripts were written. And thus the words of Jesus were selected, or invented, to sustain their Church. In this sense, not Peter's rock but Paul's pen becomes the foundation: Christianity is built on the letter, the epistle.

Congregations grew out of the Word. "In the beginning was the Word and the Word was with God, and the Word was God" (John 1:1). This Greek word *Logos* stems from a root meaning to gather, to say. Sometimes translated as reason, sometimes as speech, *Logos* is both script and voice. "And the Word was made flesh, and dwelt among us" (John 1:14). Jesus said, "Whenever two or three of you are gathered together in my name I am with you" (Matthew 18:20). Such is the meaning of the Incarnate Word. Terribly simple therefore terribly difficult. The script imparted vitality to small clusters of people who lived together in urban communes; the day began with chants and prayers at 5 a.m. (often held in catacombs, literally underground), ended with a common evening meal. We are members-one-in-another, said Paul. "And all that believed were together, and had all things in common; and sold their possessions and goods, and distributed them to all, as any had need" (Acts 2:44-45). Here then is the answer to greed, for those with courage.

These congregations, these communes, were networks united into a larger network of the Church. The network originally acted as a magnet drawing in the derelict and alienated — Christianity spread among the rabble — and those who had grown sick of Caesar. "The Roman State never attempted to educate people, only to feed and amuse them," says Ramsay, pointing out that by learning to govern themselves, to "maintain their own union through their own exertions," people were learning self-reliance. To achieve this end, Christians seized upon two great facts of the Roman world: traveling and letter-writing. "The letter [was] developed into an ideal and spiritual instrument."[25]

By means of letters, congregations expressed their mutual affection and sympathy, asking and giving counsel to each other. A collective document, the letter circulated through the congregation, was read publicly and privately, debated, discussed. On his travels Paul sent his letters ahead of him to do their work before his arrival. The letter was a spiritual position paper, written, re-written countless times in response to needs and demands of the network. Recent research on the Gnostics rather suggests that many congregations wrote their own gospels — there were perhaps dozens or even scores of gospels purporting to be the word of Jesus, a kind of anarchy the later Church found anathema.[26] But the early Church had to listen to each congregation, and the Christian epistle spoke *to* not *for* the membership. And, says Ramsay, the Church epistle was "informed and inspired with the intense personal affection which the writers felt for every individual of the thousand whom they addressed. The letter [unlike the epistle] was devoid of artificiality, spoke from the heart to the heart . . . in fact shows that the heart of man is wide enough and deep enough to entertain the same love for thousands as for one."[27] For documentation of the thesis, read again the 13th chapter of the first book of Paul's letters to the Corinthians.

Letters kept alive the Christian congregations' interest in each other, prevented excessive concentration on purely local matters and the immediate surroundings, bound all provincial churches into a Universal Church. "The Christian letters," again quoting Ramsay, "contained the saving power of the Church, and in its epistolary correspondence flowed its life blood."[28] Early bishops derived their power and position as representatives of the congregations — and were the writers and the keepers of epistles, hence the word Episcopal, from the Latin for bishop.

Thus Christianity by the time of Titus Curtisius is already growing as a counterculture within the fraying fabric of Roman society. Under Roman law the Church could have enjoyed the same religious freedom as the Jews and other sects. "Why the early Church did not fight for the same privileges is one of the legal mysteries of Christianity," says Musurillo, "and the consequences were to endure for many centuries. . . . The good Christian had been told to expect persecution, and in fact welcomed it as a test of his loyalty to the crucified Savior."[29] Thus the Christians are on their way to becoming martyrs but there are countless heroes among the masses whom history later forgot. Spartacus led a slave revolt in 73 B.C.: he put together an army of 120,000; all but 6,000 were crucified along the Appian Way, their bodies strung out for 60 miles as a deterrent to other rebellions.[30] Still in 24 A.D. there was at least one person fomenting rebellion among the slaves. This man, "a certain Titus Curtisius," Tacitus calls him, began by holding secret meetings in mountain towns and then he "published leaflets, openly calling on the country people from the remote hill pastures, and their half-savage slaves, to rise up and strike a blow for freedom."[31] The rebellion was utterly shattered by Roman troops, and Titus, a former soldier of the Praetorian Guard, along with other of the ring leaders, was returned to Rome for public execution.

That Titus Curtisius could leaflet in the mountain country off the Adriatic suggests a widespread literacy in ancient society. A mood of rebellion — even a desire for revolution — permeated the late days of Rome but the rebels could never find a uniting script. There was a pervasive disaffiliation from the dominant state and a return to an older Tribal way of life (*Fire* 72, 9-12):

> I am Hurabo, true to Bahdawils.
> Repulsed by Neurod, risking the abyss,
> We've rediscovered mountain-childhood thrills
> While on the move; sloughed off paralysis.

And by the 5th century A.D. (*Fire* 75, 9-11):

> . . . Brave, rebellious heirs of Spartacus
> Stride free but starved, while infertility
> Saps energies from sinking Rome.

The Egyptian deserts, from the earliest days, were places where criminals and tax-delinquents hid from authorities: "The native Egyptian," says Musurillo, "knew the desert and its ways so well that no Roman legionary could find him."[32] From 270 A.D. onward we hear of "men and women going off to the Egypt deserts for purely ascetic reasons . . . although communities of ascetics had existed in cities before that time. . . . Eventually, the ascetics grouped around one great leader . . . and, later, rules were drawn up," monasteries established.

Along frontiers of the Empire in the north, people went native. "Caves along the Rhone valley, unoccupied since the Stone Age," writes MacMullen, "received in the mid-third century a population of fugitives some of whom never sought out their homes again. . . . In the fourth century we meet with monks made over, or abbots reclaimed and elected, from a life of brigandage, and the leaders [of several fierce bands] eventually received veneration as saints." [33]

"I long to shatter and I long to heal."

(*Fire* 77, 11)

With all other institutions crumbling (*Fire* 79, 9-14):

> A monastery looms before our eyes:
> Stone walls which bear stark signs of many storms.
> A weathered door cracks, opens to what lies
> Within: a circle, shadows, fire-lit forms.
> > With Bahdawils here dancers celebrate
> > That fear-bred Hate we may obliterate:

Here will be preserved memories of Greece . . . that mighty catalyst. Here monks will even copy manuscripts they can no longer read. Here will be the healing journey of the inward turn (*Fire* 81, 1-14):

> My mind is racing to avoid itself;
> A swarm of high emotions makes demands.
> But intimations dawn of one true Self.

Can I now trust myself on shifting sands?
I learn to chant; my tension bends and cracks.
I breathe, breathe free, as stress is letting go;
Obsessive worries lose their grip. "Relax,"
Sings Bahdawils, "and feel your Stillness flow."
The monastery door is closing, see?
Hear sounds of clapping and of opening tombs
As Hate dissolves, turns to Serenity:
The calm of mothers' breasts and of their wombs.
    Auummmm mani padme. Peace, our breath, our One.
    Secluded flowers growing toward the sun.

E. **Script Rewritten:
   History as Transfiguration.
   (Circa 1,000 to 2,000 A.D.)**

Written symbols store information outside the brain, detach memory from protoplasm, and open the prospects for cultural transfiguration. Oral cultures remember only what they need to know for replication within their ecological niche; the script gets frozen into custom. But written script increases the chances of both evolution and extinction. Out of the silent script of mathematics came modern science — and nuclear weapons, with a technological dynamic which compels us to do what we can do, not what we should do. Weapons pile up — neutron bombs, MX missiles — while computers prepare to catapult us into outer-space, as a new generation of warriors seek the high ground. Now we follow machines as once we followed herds. Western man is a mere 3,000 years old; Neanderthalers lasted 100,000 years: Will we be so lucky?

"Winter mystery, dark force locked in ice. . ." (*Fire* 82, 1) — so seem the years between 500 and 1,000 A.D. in Europe. Intellectually, the written record is almost blank except for that strange revival of Greek and Platonism in Irish monasteries, where Erigena worked out new implications of the meaning of the word, apparently to the consternation of some of his students: they stabbed out his eyes. Europe's population dwindled from 40 million to 10 million between 200 and 900 A.D.; Rome, itself a city of a million in the 2nd century, has scarcely 20,000 by the 10th century. A theocratic form of government had replaced the municipal regime of antiquity. There were times when, as Pirenne says, "the populace was governed by its bishop and no longer asked to have the least share in that government. . ."[34] While the town of the Dark Ages had a very small resident population, it was a center of assembly, and a place of escape from marauding barbarians. Constant ravishment by the Teutons led to the construction of castles or *burgs*. In the 9th century Europe reached her lowest economic ebb, and a state of near complete political chaos. Then in the 10th century there is "a return of peace . . . a recrudescence of activity so marked that it could pass for the victorious and joyful awakening of a society long oppressed by a nightmare of anguish. There is a burst of energy . . . of optimism. The Church, revivified by the Clunisian reform, undertook to purify herself. . . . A mystic enthusiasm of which she was the inspiration animated her congregations. . . . which launched the Crusades . . ." — but also the urban revival and Cathedral building of the 11th and 12th centuries. There was a demographic revolution — Europe's population would triple between 1,000 and 1,300. "Europe colonized herself, thanks to the increase of population."[35] But behind the demographic revolution was a cultural revolution — the Cluniac movement which spear-headed the agricultural revival of Europe. Land lain fallow for centuries was reclaimed and cultivated. The monks had the organizational skills — the skills of writing script, of record-keeping — needed to turn the wilderness of Europe into a garden. By special dispensation Cluny monasteries were freed from control by the local bishops and made answerable only to the Papacy. "Cluny became a super-abbey," says Rosenstock-Hussey. "For the first time in history space was conquered by the legal personality of a corporation. . . ."[36] And for better or worse this corporation brought law and order to Western Europe in the 11th century. As an agency of pacification, Cluny by moral suasion compelled the barons to swear to uphold the "Peace of God." The Barons were made to promise not to invade churches or lay violent hands on clerics and monks. The oath read:

> I will not confiscate goods nor force the owner to repurchase them from me. . . . I will not whip peasants to make them surrender their means of life. From the kalends of May to All Saints, I will not seize horse or mare or fowl from the fields. . . . I will not make war from noon on Friday to prime on Monday.[37]

The very things which were forbidden give a glimpse of the chaos of the time. The European nobility began as a gangster class, a warrior class. A few centuries later urban populations were imposing on their kings a similar oath. A charter signed by the French king, Robert, states: "I shall rob no oxen nor other animals. . . . I shall not burn the mills, nor rob the flour. . . . I shall offer no protection to thieves."[38]

The monks of Cluny created the framework of trans-local order wherein agriculture could resume. In *Receptive to Fire* this reviving life is symbolized by Semeuse (*Fire* 85, 1-4):

> Is there reality within my trance?
> Across receptive earth Semeuse swings high,
> Her seeds in flight throughout her work and dance,
> Life-bearing arc of arm against the sky.

Here is a society in thaw: vagabondage increases; troubadours, those hippies of the 12th century, wander from town to town. To satisfy its own imperial ambition, the papacy had insisted that serfs be permitted by their masters to go on the Crusades to the Holy Land, and this active pilgrimage emancipated them, delivered the people from their spatial fixity. The Papal Court, says Rosenstock-Hussey, "broke through the forms of personal allegiance between every bishop, every abbot, every Christian and the Pope. . . . The Roman Church became the mother of every Catholic individual. The vision was not generally conceived before 1,100. It was the content of a revolution."[39] Again, for better or for worse . . .

As the Papacy moved to maximize its own power, it activated opposition to itself, stirred a sleeping population into resistance as well as adventure. The monks who made the Papal revolution are beginning to leave the monasteries, to head for the streets where they will form new orders of street preachers like the Dominicans and Franciscans. And the assertion of the rights of Mother Church — just how motherly will an all-male, 'celibate' priesthood be? — will stir new doubts, new conflict (*Fire* 86, 1-7):

> The vision fades in morning shades. Where once
> Ice formed — inflexible — clean water flows
> And Doubt, companion to Exuberance.
> Monastic grace expands, explodes, and knows
> Libidinal passion for the world,
> For conflict, creeds and freed minds clashing, Fire
> To test endurance. . .

A joyous time of contest and approaching doom. The courts of chivalric love are soon overruled by by a Pope who, determined to eliminate heretics, orders his "crusaders" in places such as Beziers and Carcassonne to simply kill everyone: "Kill all, I say! God knows His own!" (Fire 91, 10-11). A new predator is closing in with "the body of a beast, but, cruel, his face is all-too-human: sly, voracious, mauled by Greed" (*Fire* 93, 6-8). Then comes Black Death — "this killer scales our highest walls" (*Fire* 95, 9) and the religious wars of the 14th century where (*Fire* 95, 6-8):

> . . . [C]owards kill from fear,
> Still needing to control the herd, The Word
> ("Our God is One!" "No, Three!")

Fleeing this patriarchal Christian killing, the poet looks to the Mother Goddesses of the countryside . . . the witches. This older script — erotic, hallucinogenic — reaches back to the Neolithic millennia before Greco-Roman-Christo culture slid over the top of Europe. Christianity was an urban religion and until the Papal Revolution of the 12th century had been content to leave the countryside alone. Eileen Power tells how the peasant muttered charms and incantations over the fields and cattle, and the Church wisely did not interfere with the practice — it simply taught the peasant to pray to the Virgin Mary instead of Mother Earth.[40] But the more the Church extends its power, the more it activates a latent 'eroticism' of the culture[41] — there is beginning to be a rediscovery of womanhood. It can be seen in the portraiture of European art: the sexless Madonna of the 13th century gives way to the voluptuous woman of the Renaissance.[42] Hence the love scene with Semeuse (*Fire* 98, 1-14):

> A fresh day's sun on young green leaves, and blue,
> Both sea and sky, crack through our long sleep. Land.
> Your hand! I waken to the warmth of you,
> The sweetness of your body on the sand,
> Semeuse. To move, to breathe with you at last,
> Expanding, stretching, free in your embrace . . .
> "Receive, Sweet Love, our tremor and this blast
> Of soothing passion, nature's healing grace,
> Presentiment of birth we all will know."
> Arousing ocean breeze. Firm touch, moist heat,
> Volcanic surge that melted primal snow,
> Ah! Ah, Semeuse. With you I am complete.
>   The ecstasy of rise and fall: All this
>   Surpassing simple as we yield to bliss.

Here is the new script from an older time, threatening to undo the asceticism of the church. Threatening the promise of the Church. Church power derived from a pathological dread of life: Escape from this wretched vale of tears awaited the loyal in the world to come. But Bahdawils and Wanshee are symbols of an older nature-cult; here is the folk wisdom of the American Indian and the European witches. The word is derived from *wicke*, meaning wise-one. There were both female and male witches, and Wanshee, the sage, could come from either side of the Atlantic. Wanshee is rather like Castaneda's Don Juan (*Fire* 100, 1-14):

> "Reflecting light from Bahdawils, we give
> Her life for, yes, from 'cross the roughest sea
> Have travelers come to me and said, 'To live,
> Wanshee, I yearn. Give me the power to be.'

Recall the dance of Zarathustra. More:
Siddhartha's stillness dance. Recall the peace
Hurabo's people knew. Arzen restore.
Thrive, living long before the ice, then cease.
Become the sun, the moistened land. Bow! Bow
To bold Semeuse, her out-flung hand, her cheeks
Flushed, blood-rushed, seeds in flight, and be here now.
Inhale. You are the power your courage seeks.
    Just ride the wind, ride down the running stream.
    Relax. You are a dream within a dream."

Thrive . . . then cease: here is the substrate of a vigorous Sensate culture . . . a biologic mysticism, a script of life sufficient unto itself.

By the 16th century, the Church, crumbling, needed new enemies, heretics to burn. It sought out the witches, lineal descendants of Bahdawils, of the Mother Goddess Diana, and burned a million of them at the stake in the course of 150 years. Soon the burning spread to the intellectuals of the Renaissance who had by now absorbed not only Greco learning and Aristotelian logic but Arabic mathematics, the compound out of which modern science would be made. From the time of Copernicus (1473-1543) to Newton (1642-1723) a totally new conception of the physical universe would come into being. And like all truths it was bought by the blood of martyrs. Giordano Bruno, after eight years of prison can still say, "I doubt all absolutes. I doubt your way." (*Fire* 104, 10). To save his soul the Church burns his body — surely this will act as a deterrent to heresy. Instead the Church is swallowed by the fire, the Ideational Order of the Middle Ages is over, and the new Sensate is dawning (*Fire* 105, 1-14):[43]

> The aristocracy of Church and State
> Would be the center of the universe,
> So Galileo, risking Bruno's fate,
> Must also speak the doubt he feels; withstand the curse.

> For he conceives the universe a sphere
> Whose center point is everywhere, unbound,
> Evolving free: "What are the views they fear?"
> And music! Nature's harmonies resound;
> From Montaigne's tower to Shakespeare's London stage
> We mark the progress of heroic lives:
> "And readiness is all." It seems an age
> Of Reason and of Reckoning arrives.
>> Deep in his own eyes, Rembrandt finds our scope.
>> His face, our face: he reconciles our hope.

Here then is Sensate culture in its vigorous, healthy youth; here is the program which has guided the evolution of Western thought from the 17th to the 20th century whereupon it collapsed in full decay, with Galileo's progeny making bombs for Neurod:

> Our force that was deep-frozen has returned;
> Can we save and heal with powers we have learned?

(Fire 112, 13-14)

F. **Epilogue:**
    Our Generative Doubt.

This new god, Plutonium — how did it come to be, how long will it reign?

A god is only as good as its icons. As a physical object the icon calls up shared images which unite people as members of a social community. Tenth century monks pacified Europe with the icon of the cross. Out of faith in the Ideational script, the power of the Church derived. Later corrupted, the Church had undermined itself by the 16th century and in its wake came the Sensate State as the integrating political institution of western civilization. Both Church and State are 'sacred' (i.e., unquestioned) institutions held together by their *objects trouvé*, their icons. The Church uses the icon as a weapon; the State uses the weapon as an icon.

The Sensate State is grounded in a *faith in force;* its chief icon is the gun. With rifles the West was won (*Fire* 111, 5-8):

> . . . "When soldiers came
> With greed to claw and chew a 'New World,' Fear
> Repeated 'Old World' crimes; again its name
> Was Ignorance, insipid, cruel. . . ."

With guns Euro-Americans conquered the world in the heyday of Sensate culture — 1815-1914 — and then began to devour each other.[44] Pursuing peace through armed might, the Sensate States have killed some 200 million people in the 20th century — a larger number than died in the wars of all previous times. And now, armed with nuclear weapons, our leaders — our Neurods — threaten to render our planet uninhabitable.

Aware of this drift toward genocide, Norman Mayer (in 1982) seized an icon of American imperial power, the Washington Monument. Like

Hurabo, 'coming out of nowhere,' Norman acted out a script he wrote for himself. He hoped to sound an alarm, to generate dialogue . . . and was shot down by Guardians of the Peace. But he succeeded in raising the fundamental issue of our time: How can we extricate ourselves from the Sensate State?

Norman reached out, spoke truth to power, stirred doubt . . .

Only doubt can save us. This seems the most significant theme in *Receptive to Fire*: this capacity to doubt makes us human, starts the differentiation of the Omega from the Alpha Ape. But along the way of evolution the Omegas are always turning into Alphas. Even the Greeks. Even they had their idols and icons. That icon of slave-holding. To have a slave was a status-symbol, often more trouble than it was worth. Still the Greeks clung to slavery, to their master-slave script. "They were caged within the barricades of their own institutional commitments," said Alvin Gouldner. "Like men under a sentence of death, they refused to risk all in a desperate gamble, and waiting for a last reprieve which history never granted, they were dragged down to their fate."[45]

As were, in the mid-19th century, those of the Southern Confederacy. In that case, John Brown changed the course of history by attacking the icons of slavery head-on. He physically freed some slaves and physically seized a piece of ground (in Harper's Ferry) . . . thus provoking the other side into an action in defense of its icons. Property is an icon Neurod understands. Finally, our South became ridiculous even to itself. Imagine fighting and dying for the right to keep your fellow human beings in chains.

Sorokin's theory of history is predicated on the idea of the natural attrition of icons. In the Ideational order, icons symbolize the non-material, spiritual world: the bones of the saint call up images of this holy world beyond our senses . . . the world of the pure imagination. The icons of the Sensate order call forth images of the sensory world: the photographs of *Playboy* bunnies are supposed to replicate the real thing. In the Madonna painting (an icon of the Ideational world) the image does not replicate the object but paraphrases it: that is, induces your paraphrasing process, causing you to imagine an ideal relationship. (The best art, perhaps, is a fusion of the 'realistic' Sensate and the symbolic Ideational; Rembrandt's self-portraits are a perfect synthesis of idea and image.)

For a contemporary example of the transition from Sensate back to an Ideational form, hear the Jimi Hendrix rendition of the Star Spangled Banner . . . sounds of a new world. (In World War II a band leader was arrested for swinging the Star Spangled Banner: the sound was supposed to be heard from one and only one way, a Sensate way, where things sound like they are!)

In the 1960s the icons of the Sensate State lost their magic. Faith in force was undermined by a still nameless counter-faith, by doubt. Hundreds of thousands of Americans, having come to doubt the 'official' definition of reality, simply refused to participate in their State's attack on the people of Vietnam.

(Signs of the emergence of an Ideational counter-culture can be seen in the many acts of asceticism of this time. People in both Vietnam and America immolated themselves — Norman Morrison beneath Robert McNamara's window at the Pentagon.)

As the Roman Sensate State was failing, Marcus Aurelius would say (*Fire* 74, 1-4):

> "Our history, Hurabo, bends to you.
> What pledge or law could discipline your flow?
> You are a force no empire can subdue;
> The fates assign me futile tasks, I know. . . . "

The Roman icons no longer worked; no longer served to unite the people in a social network. Icons, obviously, are social: they have meaning because others impute meaning to them. The clan-emblem is the elemental icon; around it a band of people come together. An icon is the visible manifestation of a script, a story . . . It takes on meaning because it calls up a story which is believed to be true.

The famous Pax Romana was a sham: "They make a desolation and they call it Peace," said Tacitus. This was the 'peace' built on terror . . . from whence the word 'deterrence.'

Is there a peace of doubt? War is made by certainty, blind obedience. But the mind draws on dis-belief, questioning, self-examination.

Receptive to Fire is an exuberant celebration of the will to doubt (*Fire* 113, 5-6):

> . . . Certainties of outgrown creeds will crash, fall,
> Crushed by a quantum jump in consciousness. . .

And merely to utter it is to say that a new script in already forming . . . reaching back to the past . . . to go to the future.

This script contains the spark of Bahdawils . . . is that spark . . . has the power to activate life . . . the life of the mind. The poem is not about fire; it is fire . . .

Ed Powell
Buffalo, NY
January 9, 1983

ENDNOTES

1. According to *Webster's New Intercollegiate Dictionary* (1974), p. 961, *read* derives from the Middle English *reden*, to advise, interpret, akin to the Old High German *ratan* and a Greek word *arariskein*, to fit — and referred on to the verb to arm (p. 61) we find the idea of 'to carry weapons' but also to 'fortify morally.' *The Webster's Collegiate* of 1945 gives 'advise, counsel, guess' as the root meaning of the verb to read. The Oxford English Dictionary (1971), adds the idea foretell, foresee, predict . . . thus we get the reading of fortunes, dreams, etc. Suffice it here to say that we read more than marks on paper.

2. Cf. Jerome Barkow, "Attention Structure and the Evolution of Psychological Characteristics" in M. Chance and R. Larson, eds. *The Social Structure of Attention* (New York: John Wiley, 1976), 203-19, notes that as we moved toward the savannah "troop members now were dependent on each other rather than on climbing trees for protection from predators [and] would have increased the attention they paid to one another. . . [later] cooperation in hunting activities would have enhanced the troops' general level of mutual attention . . . especially toward dominant males . . . who were presumably instrumental in controlling intra-group co-operative hunting . . . and (decisively) important in ensuring that the kill was shared by other group members. Enhanced attention meant internalized representations [i.e. ideas or scripts] of greater elaborateness and longevity. Certainly by the Homo Erectus level these representations were sufficiently powerful to be attended to even in the absence of the originals themselves. For the young, this meant that mother in effect cautioned about danger even in her absence. For other members, it meant that aggression would be controlled and perhaps meat divided and other food shared even when the dominant males were not physically present. . . . These internalized representations should be thought of as proto-norms." (p. 207) Barkow assumes that "as far back as Ramapithecus [i.e., 15 myr — EHP] apes internalized representations of their fellow group members . . . and attended to these representations in the physical absence of the original." (p. 205) That is, we were trying to 'read the script of the other' (trying to anticipate what Mother would do if . . . and how to deal with the dominant male who had the power) in our imagination long, long before speech and language developed.

3   Not only primates but the whole mammalian order is defined by its sociality: cf. Peter Kropotkin, *Mutual Aid: A Factor of Evolution* (Boston: Extending Horizons, 1955), first edition in 1886, who argues that cooperation, not the competitive struggle for existence, is the propelling force of evolution.

4   C. Garth Simpson, *The Stone Age Archaeology of Southern Africa* (New York: Academic Press, 1974), 445.

5   Mark Rosenzweig, et al, "Brain Changes in Response to Experience," *Scientific American*, 226 (1972), 22-9.

6   John Pfeiffer, *The Emergence of Man* (New York: Harper Row, 1978), 94-5.

7   William Laughlin, "Hunting: An integrating Biobehavior and Its Evolutionary Importance," in R.B. Lee and I. De Vore, eds., *Symposium on Man the Hunter* (Chicago: Aldine Publishing, 1966), 304-20.

8   Carl O. Sauer, "Sedentary and Mobile Bents in Early Societies" in S. Washburn, ed., *Social Life of Early Man*, (Chicago: Aldine Publishing Co., 1961), 256-66

9   Sally Binford, "A Structural Comparison of the Dead in the Mousterian and the Upper Paleolithic," *Southwestern Journal of Anthropology* 24 (1968), 139-54.

10 "The stag-man," says Murray, "is the most important of the horned figures of the Paleolithic . . . but there are other figures . . . men with the horns of a goat or a chamois, dancing singly or in groups. . . . The art of the Paleolithic period came to a sudden and complete end before the Neolithic; it was utterly wiped out in Europe, and seems to have had no influence on later periods. The Neolithic people's figures . . . are almost invariably women, and the masked man does not appear. But when the Bronze Age is reached the horned human being is found again . . . he plays a flute and is in the midst of animals." Margaret Murray, *The God of the Witches* (New York: Doubleday Anchor Books, 1969), 15-21.

11 Otto Jesperson, *Language: Its Nature, Development and Origins* (New York: 1921), 432-7.

12 Nancy Tanner and Adrienne Zihlman, "Discussion Paper: Evolution of Human Communication: What Can Primates Tell Us?" *The Annals of the New York Academy of Sciences*, 280 (1976) 467-80.

13 Paul Shepard, *The Tender Carnivore and the Sacred Game* (New York: Charles Scribners, 1973), 165-66.

14 Julian Jaynes, *The Origins of Consciousness in the Breakdown of the Bicameral Mind* (Boston: Houghton Mifflin, 1976), 97.

15 Elizabeth Gould Davis, *The First Sex*, (New York: G. P. Putnam, 1971) 40-41, et passim.

16 A. Moret and G. Davy, *From Tribe to Empire: Social Organization among Primitives and in the Ancient East* (New York: Alfred A. Knopf, 1926), 124-26.

17 Fustel de Coulanges, *The Ancient City: A Study on the Religion, Laws and Institutions of Greece and Rome* (New York: Doubleday Anchor, 1956, first edition, 1864.) Coulanges was Durkheim's mentor, for whom the *Division of Labor* was written as a Ph.D.

18 Jaynes, op. cit., 212, "The collapse of the bicameral mind was certainly accelerated by this collapse under the ocean of a good part of the Aegean people's land . . . with air shock waves estimated at 350 times more powerful than the hydrogen bomb."

19 *Ibid.*, 97-99.

20 W. M. Ramsay, *The Letters to the Seven Churches of Asia and Their Place in the Plan of the Apocalypse* (New York: A. C. Armstrong, 1905) 1-4, et passim.

21 *Ibid.*

22 Elwin H. Powell, "Anomie and Force: The Case of Rome," *Catalyst* (Spring, 1969), 79-101.

23 Karl Kautsky, *Foundations of Christianity: A Study of Christian Origins* (New York: Monthly Review, 1972). First Edition 1925. Kautsky, a leader of the German Socialists, died in a Nazi concentration camp. Citations pp. 114-16.

24 *Ibid.*

25 Ramsay, op. cit., 1-15, et passim.

26 Elaine Pagels, *The Gnostic Gospels* (New York: Random House, 1979).

27 Ramsay, *op. cit.*

28 *Ibid.*, 29.

29 Herbert A. Musurillo, SJ., *The Fathers of the Primitive Church* (New York: A Mentor-Omega Book, 1966), 19

30 Powell, *op. cit.*, 80

31 *The Annals of Tacitus, A New Translation by D. R. Dudley* (New York: Mentor, 1966), 155.

32 Musurillo, *op. cit.*, 27.

33 Ramsay MacMullen, *Enemies of the Roman Order: Treason, Unrest, and Alienation in the Empire* (Cambridge: Harvard University Press, 1966), 196.

34 Henri Pirenne, *Medieval Cities* (Princeton University Press, 1939).

35 *Ibid.*

36 Eugene Rosenstock-Hussey, *The Driving Power of Western Civilization* (Boston: Beacon Press, 1951).

37 William E. Brown, *The Achievement of the Middle Ages* (Edinburgh: Sands and Co., 1928), 88. Cf. also, Charles Homer Haskins, *The Renaissance of the Twelfth Century* (Cambridge: Harvard University Press, 1929), 15, et. passim.

38 As quoted by Kropotkin, *op. cit.*

39 Rosenstock-Hussey, *op. cit.*

40 Eileen Power, *Medieval People* (New York: Doubleday Anchor, 1954).

41 Alan Gunn, *The Mirror of Love: A Reinterpretation of the Romance of the Rose* (Lubbock, Texas: Texas Technological College Press, 1952).

42 P.S. Sorokin, *Social and Cultural Dynamics: Fluctuations of Forms in Art,* Vol. I. (Painting, Sculpture, Architecture, Music, Literature and Criticism) (New York: Bedminster Press, 1962), p. 489 shows that the proportion of male to female figures in portraiture changes as follows: X century=89% male, 11% female; X-XI=83-17; XII-XIII=81-19; XIV-XV= 75-25; XVI=59-41; XVII=62-38; XVIII=65-35; XIX=62-38; XX=62-38.

43 In four volumes — some 4,000 pages — Sorokin has analyzed the rise and fall of western civilization through two "super-cycles" of movement: Ideational to Idealistic to Sensate culture and then back again. Now at the end of the Sensate cycle, Sorokin predicted (in the 1930s) that a new Ideational order would soon emerge. Elements of that prophesy came to pass in the counterculture of the 1960s, and in the upsurging mysticism of the psychedelic movement. In 116 stanzas *Receptive to Fire* tells the same story. There are different ways of knowing, and different ways of saying.

44 Elwin H. Powell, *The Design of Discord: Studies of Anomie* (New York: Oxford University Press, 1970), 149, *et passim*.

45 Alvin W. Gouldner, *Enter Plato: Classical Greece and the Origins of Social Theory* (New York: Basic Books, 1965).

GLOSSARY

Ahimsa [112]: To do no harm; to practice kindness and non-violence toward all living things. A word derived from Sanskrit, ahimsa was a key element of the avowed values and practices of Mohandas Gandhi.

Akhenáten [47]: A Pharaoh of Egypt's 18th dynasty, Akhenáten died young (c. 1336 BC) after a 17-year reign during which he abandoned traditional Egyptian polytheism in favor of worship of the god Aten alone. Some see this as a precursor of monotheistic practices that would arise (with predictable consequences of dogmatism) elsewhere in the world. Not long after Akhenáten's death, the old gods in Egypt regained their status.

Anarchy [45]: Built on compassion and respect, a philosophy of living that strives for a sharing of power among all the world's people.

Antinoüs [71]: In 130 BC, the young Antinoüs drowned in the river Nile, perhaps during a trip with his lover, the Roman Emperor, Hadrian, who later deified him.

Aum mani padme [81]: A mantra intended to direct our attention to the infinite compassion and light that many Buddhists believe is at the essence of each of us.

Bruno [104]: An Italian Dominican friar born in 1548, Giordano Bruno was burned at the stake in 1600 for having dared to suggest that our Sun might be a star and the universe infinite.

Danube [71]: At the time of Julius Caesar [1st century BC] and for many centuries thereafter, a major Roman project was to try to keep Germanic tribes from crossing the Danube, a boundary of the Empire.

Don Juan & Figaro [106]: In his operas, *Figaro* (1786) and *Don Giovanni* (1787) the "genius boy," Mozart, prefigured the French Revolution of 1789.

***Fidelio* [110]**: Beethoven's 1805 opera in praise of Revolutionary courage. In order to free her imprisoned lover, the heroine, Leonore, poses as a man, Fidelio.

Golden Flower [96]: For Chinese Daoists, an image related to the idea of our original – and immortal – essence.

Gracchi Brothers [70]: The brothers, Tiberius and Gaius, were Roman Plebian nobles who, while serving as tribunes in the 2nd century BC, attempted to pass land reform legislation that would redistribute major patrician landholdings among the plebeians. Because these and other challenges to business-as-usual threatened the tight grip of Imperial power structures, both were assassinated, a history-changing tragedy repeated two millennia later – and for the same reasons – when the Kennedy brothers, John and Robert, challenged the American Empire. Many historians consider the Gracchi to be the founding fathers of both socialism and populism.

Hamāsah [88-9]: Arabic word carrying the meaning of both enthusiasm and fortitude.

***I Ching* [26, 35]**: This classic Chinese text dates from the mid-4th to early-3rd centuries BC, though archeological work turns up its origins thousands of years before that time. Also known as the Book of Changes, it is widely used as a divination system, but commentaries – both Eastern and Western – offered throughout the centuries have also made it a fascinating and valuable book of philosophy.

Isaac [68]: In the story revered by three of the world's "great religions," Abraham is willing to sacrifice his son, Isaac, to God.

Melos [58]: The Greek historian Thucydides wrote that, in 416 BC, Athens attacked Melos for refusing to submit tribute and refusing to join Athens' alliance against Sparta. The victorious Athenians executed all of the adult men of Melos and sold the women and children into slavery, a common practice during this period that many consider a high point of Western Civilization.

Mihiragula, Mahmud, Khan [96]: Among the leaders of several ancient invasions and mass migrations of Central Asian tribes that caused chaos, particularly in areas of modern day India and Pakistan around the Punjab.

Nagasaki [112]: On August 8, 1945, three days after obliterating Hiroshima, and not even having the compassion or decency to give Japan's surviving people time to arrange to surrender, United States leaders chose to drop a second atomic bomb, incinerating tens of thousands of the women, men, and children of Nagasaki.

Plutonium [112]: Among the many "waste products" created in every nuclear power plant and released into the atmosphere thru every leak, every accident, and of course in every stage of the production and use of nuclear weapons (including the so-called "uranium-tipped" weapons now being regularly used around the world by the U.S. military), Plutonium 239 is our world's most dangerous and cancer-creating substance. Its "half-life" of 24,000 years means that half of it will still have not decayed during that length of time, and that, if there is still life on our planet, the plutonium will still be with us, creating cancers. 48,000 years into the future, one-quarter of it will be doing the same. Etcetera. Etcetera. So, yes, for all practical purposes, "Plutonium is forever."

Polyxena [43]: In many Greek and Roman myths about Priam and Hecuba, king and queen of Troy, Polyxena is mentioned as one of their daughters. In some of the stories, it is Odysseus who leads her to her death as a sacrifice to the gods.

riverrun [96]: The last word of James Joyce's *Finnegans Wake* connects to this (lowercase) opening word of the novel.

Savonarola [103]: Known in Florence for his book burning and destruction of what he considered immoral art, Savonarola [1452-1498] preached that the world would be coming to an end in 1500, but it was Savonarola's own life that came to an end, through execution, in 1498.

Shiva [48]: A major Hindu deity. In various traditions, Shiva is regarded as the Supreme God or as one of the primary forms of God. Represented as a handsome young man immersed in deep meditation or dancing upon the demon of ignorance, it is said that Shiva retains an appearance of eternal youth because of his authority over death, rebirth and immortality.

Siddhartha: Throughout *Receptive to Fire*, Siddhartha is based loosely on the prince who became, in Buddhist mythology, the historical Buddha.

Simrand [20, 111]: A mythical region of sub-Saharan Africa.

Tat tvam asi [39]: Originally occurring in the Chandogya Upanishad, this Vedic Sanskrit sentence conveys the belief that The Self, in its primordial state, is identical with the ground and origin of all phenomena; and that the knowledge that this is so may characterize the experience of liberation.

Thersites [59]: His story in *The Iliad* is unique: A "commoner" in an army dominated by aristocrats, Thersites dared challenge the supreme commander, Agamemnon.

Tikkun Olam [47]: A Hebrew phrase sometimes translated as "repairing the world." In a prayer attributed to the Biblical Joshua, God is praised for allowing the Jewish people to serve Him. In today's progressive forms of Judaism we find in Tikkun Olam a commitment to bringing about a world in which love and mercy reign for all.

Vedas [48]: Arising among Indo-Aryan people c. 1500 BC in areas surrounding what is now Northern India and continuing to evolve during the period from 500 to 400 BC, Vedic texts were transmitted by oral tradition alone until the rise of Buddhism during the 1st century BC, at which time a literary tradition set in. At the culmination of Chinese traditions that had developed during the same period as the Vedas, the first verse of Laotsu's text, the Dao de Ching, tells us that the Dao is that which cannot be named and that, when we try to name it, it slips through our fingers. In saying "Truth is One, the wise call it by many names," it seems to me that the Vedas come close to this same central agnostic understanding.

Yin & Yang [49]: Dating back perhaps 5,000 years in Chinese philosophy, the concept of yin yang describes polar or seemingly contrary forces – dark/light, soft/hard, cold/hot – as interconnected and interdependent in the natural world; two aspects of a single reality, each containing the seed of the other. Yin & Yang do not merely replace each other but become one another through the constant flow of the universe, a concept also expressed in various African variants.

In tai chi as a martial art, yielding is found to be a force as powerful as aggression, but in popular culture yielding is often mistaken as passivity (sexual and otherwise). To match dark, cold, and yielding as female with bright, hot and forceful as male can be quite misleading, so I prefer to emphasize the reality that we men and women become more complete by developing both aspects of this single reality – yin/yang – within ourselves.

Zarathustra: While appearing throughout *Receptive to Fire*, Zarathustra is based not so much on the perhaps-mythical Persian hero, but loosely on the central character in Nietzsche's poem, "Thus Spoke Zarathustra."

ALSO AVAILABLE FROM
COLLEGE CITY PUBLICATIONS!

B Wardlaw's
Coca-Cola Anarchist

THE STORY BEHIND THE
CREATION OF *RECEPTIVE TO FIRE*

**To read an excerpt,
see pages 122 and 123.**

For more information and to order online,
visit: http://cocacolaanarchist.com

FROM *COCA-COLA ANARCHIST*, CHAPTER ONE

Who Will Wash the Dishes?

WITH A PUSH OF MEMORY AND WORDS, I'm opening a heavy door resting on old hinges. It swings out onto the Atlanta of my childhood, teeming with secrets both communal and private.

My voice is the voice of a truant, a bad boy, a wayward son who has come home. I grew up rich, white, and, as far back as I can remember, angry. Anger is demanding but elusive; it takes us on unpredictable journeys. When blocked, it dodges, feints, dissimulates. Like flowing water, it will find release.

In my Atlanta, "nice people" tried not to show anger, extreme joy, or — God forbid! — sensuality. Waves of forbidden emotions broke through as frustration and sadness. Muscles rippling in my father's clenched jaw. Volumes spoken through my mother's depressed silences. I left home at many ages and in many styles, but always I came back, wondering if I could find clues as to where I might belong.

Like anger, change finds its way. In Atlanta, today, there is no holding back change for any of us — our rich, not-so-rich, and poor; our people of many shades of black, brown, and beige. Change, both public and private. Hope, both public and private. Male in a violently male-dominated society, I need to speak of these changes of which I am a part.

As with Chambers of Commerce the world over, Atlanta's has long aspired for our city to be seen as progressive and sophisticated. An international destination. In our case, perhaps even a New York of the South. But in the early 1990s city leaders awakened to the unsettling fact that, in hosting the '96 Olympic Games, Atlanta's soft underbelly would be dramatically exposed. Forgetting or ignoring that all the world has poverty and could benefit from dealing with the scourge, head-on, those who were calling the shots felt they needed to hide the truth about Atlanta's economic condition and our particular shame: the fact that hugely disproportionate numbers of our impoverished are descendants of the very slaves on whose backs our revered South was built. Marked out in the 1830s as a railroad terminal, our city had been a crossroad not so much on the underground railways through which slaves escaped, but on the above-ground ones where slaves were moved around as chattel. Atlanta's financially motivated pre-Olympic instinct was to sanitize the Peachtree Corridor, a wide swath of primarily white Atlanta most vulnerable to being scrutinized by the world. "Sanitize" meant: "Sweep the bums, the panhandlers, the destitute, and unsightly from this area where visitors will be spending most of their time and money."

...By the time I reached my early twenties, I had stopped calling Atlanta "home," and yet I was continually pulled back. The '96 Olympics seduced me into taking a new look, deeper, more extensive. In the 1860s, a serious question in Atlanta, and in much of the world, was, "Should some people be able to own other people as slaves?" In the 1990s, advocates for Atlanta's homeless, along with much of the world, were asking, "Should some people enjoy extravagant luxury while others live in the virtual slavery of economic poverty?" Every night, thousands of men, women, and children — some working, some unemployed, some "unemployable" — were trying to survive, homeless, in our city. Mother, widowed but inspiringly alert in her late-eighties, listened as I, pushing toward sixty, talked with her about the pre-Olympic sanitizing and the devastating effect it was having on Atlanta's poor.

For most of my life, it had certainly seemed unlikely that my mother and I would ever see eye-to-eye. But now, beyond our personal travails and six months after the Olympics, the Southern belle who had long tried to make a safe and proper home for her family, and I, the rich boy who, in her home, had felt out of place, felt "homeless," formed a partnership. As Olympic dust began to settle, leaving Atlanta with even less affordable housing than in the inadequate days before the Games, we came together and, through one of our family foundations, bought a 96,000-square-foot building on Peachtree Street for Atlanta's Task Force for the Homeless...

For more information, visit: http://cocacolaanarchist.com

www.ingramcontent.com/pod-product-compliance
Lightning Source LLC
Chambersburg PA
CBHW050558300426
44112CB00013B/1981